The Rule of Reverse Results

Do extreme, unethical governmental policies often produce results opposite to those intended? This book considers the ironic outcomes of recent global events and concludes that there is a 'rule of reverse results' at work. While not a hard and fast law, the rule points out the increased probability that a policy will backfire if it is immoral while ethical policies, even if extreme, are unlikely to produce reverse results. The issue here is that of increased likelihood but not of certainty. Governments can never be sure as to the effects of their actions: to some extent they are always working in the dark. But if the motivation is right, moral and humane the policies will not often produce adverse results the opposite of those intended. Based on events in global history in the Twentieth and Twenty-First centuries the chapters can each be read individually, as well as being part of the argument.

Audrey Wells, Royal Holloway College, University of London, UK.

The Rule of Reverse Results

The effects of unethical policies?

Audrey Wells

Routledge
Taylor & Francis Group

LONDON AND NEW YORK

First published 2016
by Routledge
2 Park Square, Milton Park, Abingdon, Oxon OX14 4RN

and by Routledge
605 Third Avenue, New York, NY 10017

First issued in paperback 2021

*Routledge is an imprint of the Taylor & Francis Group, an
informa business*

British Library Cataloguing in Publication Data
A catalogue record for this book is available from the British Library

Library of Congress Cataloging-in-Publication Data
Names: Wells, Audrey, author.
Title: The rule of reverse results : the effects of unethical policies? /
   by Audrey Wells.
Description: Burlington, VT : Ashgate, 2016. | Includes bibliographical
   references and index.
Identifiers: LCCN 2015045528 | ISBN 9781472485465 (hardback :
   alk. paper)
Subjects: LCSH: Political ethics. | International relations—Moral and
   ethical aspects. | World politics—20th century—Moral and ethical
   aspects. | World politics—21st century—Moral and ethical aspects.
Classification: LCC JA79 .W39 2016 | DDC 172/.4—dc23
LC record available at http://lccn.loc.gov/2015045528

ISBN 13: 978-1-03-209789-3 (pbk)
ISBN 13: 978-1-4724-8546-5 (hbk)

Typeset in Times New Roman
by Apex CoVantage, LLC

To
Bernard, Howard, Diana and Peter
with love and gratitude

Contents

Introduction

In this book I consider the ironic outcomes of recent global events and conclude that there is a 'rule of reverse results' whereby extreme, unethical governmental policies often produce results opposite to those intended. This rule is not a hard and fast law, but one of the increased probability that a policy will backfire if it is immoral in the sense of causing unnecessary suffering, particularly loss of life. On the other hand, ethical policies, even if extreme, are unlikely to produce reverse results. The issue here is that of increased likelihood but not of certainty.

Governments can never be sure, of course, as to the effects of their actions. But if the motivation is right, moral and humane the policies will not often produce adverse results, the opposite of those intended. Whether this rule may also be applied to our personal lives cannot be considered here, but it may indeed be so.

The concept of the rule of reverse results partly resembles the law of unintended consequences, which was first analysed by Robert K. Merton in his 'The Unanticipated Consequences of Purposive Social Action', published in 1936. He identified five sources of unanticipated consequences: ignorance, error, immediate interests which may override long-term interests, basic values (as when the Protestant work ethic results in the accumulation of such wealth that work is unnecessary) and self-defeating prediction (as when a prediction of mass starvation prompts increased agricultural production).

The rule of reverse results, however, partly differs from the law of unintended consequences in that the former is concerned only with unethical actions, which often result in the complete opposite of the intended outcome. As such the rule is an additional argument, besides the waste of life and money, against the use of military force or extremely harsh policies unless they are clearly justified on moral grounds.

My argument is also not the same as that of Chalmers Johnson in his book *Blowback*, published in 2000. He was mainly concerned with the revenge taken against the USA by victims of American foreign policy. The term 'blowback' was used in war when poison gas meant for the enemy was unexpectedly blown back by the senders. The word was then used by the CIA when their covert actions resulted in their victims' attacking an American embassy, for example. The American public would be shocked and ignorant of the cause of the attack, which the CIA would call 'blowback'. My study is more global in its subject matter than that of Chalmers Johnson, and concerned not only with acts of revenge but also with unethical actions by governments that have resulted in the reverse of what was intended.

The book is based on a number of events in global history in the twentieth and twenty-first centuries. To aid comprehension the chapters are grouped into headed sections, but they can each be read as independent of the others and in any order, as well as being part of the argument. As such the book also becomes a short guide to certain issues in international affairs.

I have explored in detail each example to back up my argument that extremely unethical policies are likely to produce reverse results, while extremely ethical policies often not only succeed far beyond original hopes but also prevent the reverse results from other people's evil policies. I have in addition considered examples which do not support my argument but have concluded that while the rule of reverse results does not always apply, it does so with a frequency worth examining as a recognisable pattern.

The study begins with an analysis of how Israel has undermined its own security by its treatment of the Palestinians. Insecurity is the last thing it wants. Its main ally, the USA, has also jeopardised its security by backing Israel to the detriment of the well-being of the Palestinians. American uncritical support of Israel and involvement in Muslim countries have helped make the USA the target of Islamic terrorism.

The second section deals with Western military interventions in Islamic countries during the twentieth and twenty-first centuries, which have certainly triggered reverse results. The interventions were unethical in so far as they caused unnecessary suffering and loss of life, or were for commercial or national self-interest, as well as being ill-informed, without reconstruction planning and against the wishes of some members of the UN Security Council.

In Iran, if Britain and the USA had not toppled Mossadeq in 1953, the revolution of 1979, exporting Islamic extremism, would most probably never have taken place, nor, without its financial and military support, could Hezbollah and Hamas have flourished.

In Iraq in 2003, the overthrow of Saddam Hussein, by mainly American and British troops without UN authorisation, opened the door to al-Qaeda, against which Saddam had been a bulwark. Chaos and violence ensued, ultimately threatening the West and leading to the rise of ISIS.

The results of Western intervention in both Iran and Iraq were, of course, the last thing that the USA and Britain had wanted in those countries.

In Afghanistan the USA's training of Muslim militants against the USSR backfired when they attacked America because of its foreign policy in the Middle East. The military response of the USA and its allies to the 9/11 attack did not produce the desired result either as it increased support for the Taleban in Pakistan. Moreover, although Osama bin Laden was killed, al-Qaeda was not destroyed but simply relocated.

In Libya the overthrow of Gaddafi meant the foreseeable rise of the Islamic extremists which he was attempting to crush. Furthermore, the resulting paralysis in the UN after the Libyan conflict exacerbated the difficulties in negotiating peace talks over Syria.

Section 3 is concerned with China and Russia, which both experienced the extremism of communism. In China, after coming to power in 1949, the Communists introduced socialist reforms which greatly improved the lives of the poor but, after a decade, the programme became too extreme and harsh in Mao's hands. His policies of the Great Leap and the Cultural Revolution resulted in the Chinese government's moving radically away from them to implement capitalism after his death, which was the last thing he would have wanted.

In Russia, Stalin sowed the seeds of the eventual collapse of the Soviet Union with his brutal policies of collectivised agriculture and imposing the ring of buffer states in Eastern Europe.

Section 4 concerns the Second World War, which was not inevitable but its likelihood greatly increased by France's taking revenge on Germany with the Treaty of Versailles in 1919. This eventually contributed to France's defeat and occupation by the Nazis in 1940. In that year Britain retaliated for the Luftwaffe's mistaken bombing of civilian areas in London (which was against Hitler's orders) with the bombing of Berlin. The Nazis responded with the Blitz.

One of the gravest crimes against humanity is considered in the next section: genocide, the deliberate attempt to destroy an ethnic group. It certainly backfired in the hands of Hitler and the Nazis as they actually created inadvertently the state of Israel, the last thing they wanted, by making Jews more conscious of their identity and forcing them to flee from Europe in large numbers. The Haavara Agreement encouraged them to go to Palestine. Thus the Nazis' persecution, which was clearly evil, resulted in the complete opposite of their goal.

In Bosnia and Kosovo the results were not so dramatic, but genocide certainly did not produce a Greater Serbia as the Serbs had wanted. Both countries became independent while some of the leading perpetrators of the massacres ended up imprisoned by International Criminal Tribunals.

NATO's intervention in Bosnia and Kosovo, on the other hand, was rightly motivated and did not lead to negative unintended consequences.

Of course the outcome of an evil policy is not always that the results are the reverse of those intended. There is an increased likelihood that they will be if the intention is unethical but not a certainty. I therefore have also considered examples of where the rule of reverse results has not seemed to apply, as in Rwanda, Cambodia, Sri Lanka, Darfur and ISIS, as well as the USA's interventions in Latin America. (In Cuba, however, the USA's policy did backfire, driving Castro straight into the arms of the USSR.) European imperialism does not seem to have produced many reverse results, but sometimes these were avoided by ethical leaders of resistance movements, guiding the people away from revenge to forgiveness and reconciliation.

Noble, moral and compassionate policies, while they may be extreme, do not produce reverse results and can indeed have a countervailing effect on evil policies, preventing them from backfiring on the perpetrators. Nelson Mandela's policy of reconciliation after the end of apartheid was a good example of this, as was the French foreign minister Robert Schuman's desire to forgive Germany and work with it to create peace through the European Coal and Steel Community, which grew into the EU. In India, Gandhi's policy of non-violent resistance against the British won the world's lasting admiration.

My conclusion from this study of policies which can be deemed extremely unethical or harsh is that there is a rule of reverse results in the sense that such policies have a greater likelihood of being counterproductive. Some might see in this pattern a dialectic at work, swinging from thesis to antithesis, going to the wires and then boomeranging. But in fact in most of these cases it is the human will that has been forced to respond in an extreme way to an extreme situation created by others.

Political events are confluences of many factors and involve people with free will to make choices. As a result it is impossible to predict an event with absolute certainty or to argue that it was inevitable. But there are nevertheless some policies which are more likely to become counterproductive than others. Military intervention in a foreign country usually destabilises it and produces a nationalist backlash, policies of revenge backfire, unrelieved poverty encourages support for extremist movements, such as communism or more recently Islamism, genocide usually fails and its perpetrators usually jailed.

The diplomacy of forgiveness, persistence in peace negotiations, and caring for the poor, if practised on the world stage, would do much to avoid the rule of reverse results occurring. These ethical principles are considered in the conclusion.

Countless lives could be saved if these principles were practised. The West's involvement in the Middle East exemplifies what happens when they are not. We shall therefore begin with a consideration of Israel's counterproductive search for security.

Section 1

Israel

1 Israel has caused its own insecurity together with that of the USA

The resurrection of ancient Israel after centuries of Jewish suffering has often been regarded as one of the greatest events of the twentieth century. At last it seemed that the Jews would have their own state, a permanent haven from persecution. However, in their search for security the Israelis seized the land of the Palestinians, whose consequent attacks on Israel have denied its citizens the very security for which they still long. As the years have passed and the Palestinians' grievances have been neglected, increasingly lethal Islamic groups, such as Hamas and Hezbollah, have developed to end the Palestinians' suffering. More recently al-Qaeda took up their cause, which was one of the expressed reasons for its attack on Israel's main ally, the USA, on 11 September 2001.[1] Indeed, the security of much of the world is now threatened by the conflict between Israel and the Palestinians.

Israel's brutal treatment of the Palestinians has shocked the international community, prompting many Israelis themselves to condemn it. The Israeli historian Avi Shlaim has highlighted an important issue: 'The death and destruction inflicted by Israel on the innocent civilians of Gaza raises a question: how does a people that has been the victim of such indescribable callousness come to be the cruel tormentor of another people?'[2] His answer is that in the 1920s the hard-line Zionists developed the doctrine of the 'Iron Wall', whereby they always had to deal with the Palestinians from a position of military strength. This doctrine became central to Israeli policy.[3]

An additional argument might be that Israel in the 1940s was created more from the Jews' desire to escape persecution rather than from a positive desire to create a state based on Jewish ideals and ethics. Therefore many Jews became militantly obsessed with security to the exclusion of compassion towards the Palestinians.

Furthermore, during the Second World War, the West did not help the Jewish refugees as it might have done, thus contributing later to the Israelis' belief that they had to look after themselves as no one else would do so. Therefore Britain and the USA, as well as Germany, must bear some of the blame for Israel's aggressive search for security, which must be seen in its wider historical context.

Today American support of Israel has enabled it to oppress the Palestinians. Consequently the USA has been criticised worldwide and has been violently attacked by Muslim extremists.

Whatever the reason for Israel's harsh treatment of the Palestinians, it is clear that it has been counterproductive, undermining the very security for which the Israelis have longed. Religious Jews seem ironically the most hard-line. Indeed, there seems to be an absence in Israel of rabbis who will speak out loudly, like the prophets of old, condemning 'the Chosen People' for their unethical behaviour.

The Arabs also warrant criticism since the oil-rich Arab countries have not helped the Palestinians as they might have done and the Palestinians have not been well organised or led, nor have their leaders been above corruption. Furthermore all the Palestinian leaders should have been more open to negotiation and compromise. Nevertheless it is Israel's oppressive occupation of the lands of the Palestinians that is the reason for the latter's regularly attacking it with rockets or suicide bombers.

I shall now examine the four reasons for Israel's insecurity for which it is responsible: first its occupation of former Palestinian lands, second the consequent growth of increasingly lethal pro-Palestinian organisations, third Israel's political parties and fourth its acceptance of military, financial and diplomatic support from the USA.

Israel's occupation of former Palestinian lands

When in November 1947, the UN voted to partition Palestine, creating a Jewish state, an Arab state and a UN administered Jerusalem, the Jews accepted the plan but the Arabs did not, believing it to be unfair as it allocated 56 per cent of its land to the Jews, who made up only a third of its population. The Arabs, in any case, wanted a united state. Conflict intensified between the Arabs and Jews in Palestine, ending with Jews triumphing.

Israel emerges 1948 – Palestine disappears

On 14 May 1948, when the British Mandate expired, Israel declared its independence. The next day neighbouring Arab states attacked Israel on behalf of the Palestinians. As the Arabs had fewer troops and were disunited and incompetent, they lost to Israel. In 1949, when the UN secured armistice agreements between Israel and Egypt and the Arab states, almost half of the Palestinian Arabs – that is, 725,000 people – had become refugees. This was the result partly of force but also of fear, caused by reports of massacres, such as that at Deir Yassin, where 250 Palestinians were killed by the Irgun (a Zionist paramilitary group) on 10 May 1948. Some of the Palestinians fled to other Arab countries, others to the unconquered areas of Palestine, the West Bank and the Gaza Strip, which came under the control of Jordan and Egypt respectively. Palestine disappeared, but not in the minds of the Palestinians, who call the events at this time 'al-Nakba', or 'the disaster', while the Israelis call it the 'war of independence'.

There have been in fact two versions of these events, the official Israeli one and that of the Arabs. According to the former account, justifying Israel's occupation, the Arabs left their lands of their own accord, believing they would regain them later. According to the latter version the Arabs were forcibly expelled from their homes. It was not until the 1980s and the opening of the official Israeli archives that the truth emerged, due to research by such Israeli historians as Benny Morris. He argued that while there was no centralised policy of expulsion, the Israeli high command did actually order expulsions to their requirements. Of the 228 empty Palestinian villages that he studied, he found that in 41 of them the Israeli Defence Force had ordered the expulsions and in 90 the residents had fled because of attacks on other villages. Only in six of the villages did the residents in fact leave due to orders from the local Palestinian authorities. He was unable to account for the evacuation of the other villages.[4]

Although the UN recommended that the refugees wishing to return to their homes and live in peace with their neighbours should be permitted to do so, Israel would not allow this, seizing the land and property of the Palestinian refugees. For their part, the Arab states refused to recognise Israel, which, although extending its territory, felt the need to remain on a war footing, constantly feeling vulnerable.

The Six-Day War

The first Israeli-Arab war in 1948–49, when the Israelis forcefully expelled or frightened Palestinians into fleeing from their land, was seen by the Israelis as a 'defensive' war. This how they also called their subsequent wars, which actually weakened their defence by intensifying Arab hostility. These wars were the Suez War in 1956, the Six-Day War in 1967 and the Yom Kippur War in 1973.

It was the Six-Day War that enabled Israel to occupy the Gaza Strip, the West Bank and East Jerusalem, as well as the Golan Heights and Sinai Peninsula: conquests that guaranteed Israel's insecurity. Israel had begun it. Fearing an imminent attack, on 5 June 1967 Israel made a pre-emptive strike against the Egyptian airfields, and then attacked Jordan and Syria, Egypt's allies. Within a few hours Israel spectacularly destroyed 90 per cent of the Egyptian air force, about 70 per cent of the Syrian air force and almost all of the Jordanian air force.

After six days the war was over. Israel had taken control of the Sinai Peninsula from Egypt, the Golan Heights from Syria, a strip of land on the Jordanian frontier and the territories populated with Palestinian refugees: the West Bank, the Gaza Strip and East Jerusalem.

UN Resolution 242

The UN therefore tried to resolve the situation. In November 1967 the Security Council agreed on its Resolution 242, which basically proposed 'land for peace': that Israel would get peace in exchange for the Arab lands it had taken. The UN Security Council called for the withdrawal of Israeli forces 'from territories occupied in the recent conflict'. The words 'all the' before the word 'territories' were deliberately omitted.[5] The resolution was formulated by Lord Caradon, the British ambassador to the UN, who rejected the Soviet demand that the words 'all the' be included before the word 'territories' to avoid alienating Israel.

The resolution also called for respect for the right of all Middle Eastern states 'to live in peace within secure and recognised boundaries' but did not clarify precisely what was meant by the phrase. As a result Israel argued that as it also needs 'secure and recognised boundaries' the resolution could not mean it had to return to its borders in 1949, whereas Egypt, Jordan and Lebanon, which were Arab countries that accepted the resolution, asserted that Israel must give up its conquered territories, emphasising the resolution's preamble, referring to the 'inadmissibility of the acquisition of territory by war'.

Thus Resolution 242, like the Balfour Declaration, was framed in the finest tradition of British diplomatic ambiguity so that it gained the unanimous support of the Security Council as members interpreted it differently. Later on, of course, problems developed with regard to its meaning. Since Israel has refused to withdraw to the pre-1967 borders, there has been inconclusive debate over whether Israel is in contravention of international law depending on the interpretation of Resolution 242.

As to the victims of the war, disgracefully the resolution did not even refer to the Palestinians by name, only indirectly calling for a solution to the refugee problem.

Israel's occupation of the Gaza Strip, the West Bank and East Jerusalem since 1967

After 1967 thousands of Israelis went to settle in the Occupied Territories, often bulldozing the homes of the Palestinians and taking away their lands. To make matters worse, many Palestinian farmers found they could no longer make a living through farming as they were denied the subsidies enjoyed by

Israeli farmers, who flooded the Palestinian market with their cheap agricultural produce. Furthermore restrictions on land use and access to the Israeli markets destroyed the livelihoods of the Palestinian farmers, who were often forced to travel each day to take low-paid manual jobs in Israel. By the time of the First Intifada, despite possessing higher educational qualifications, 40 per cent of the Palestinian workforce had to work for the Israelis in unskilled or semi-skilled jobs which the Israelis did not want to do.

The First Intifada 1987

In 1987, after twenty years of Israeli oppression, including extrajudicial killings, mass detentions, house demolitions and forced relocations, Palestinians rose up in the 'intifada' or 'uprising' against Israel's rule in the Occupied Territories. Mainly young Palestinians pelted armed Israeli patrols with stones and petrol bombs. Arab workers went on strike and Arab traders closed their businesses. The 'intifada' was widely supported by the Palestinians. The Israeli army was sent in to restore order, but it was not until 1991 that the 'intifada' died down. By then, well-publicised photographs of Israeli soldiers beating children and firing on crowds of young Palestinians, some of whom were killed, had lost Israel the support of world opinion, which had swung in favour of the Palestinians.

Gaza under siege

As I shall explain later, in 2007 Israel imposed a blockade against Gaza, which had been taken over by the extremist organisation Hamas. As a result of this and Egypt's sealing the tunnels, the Palestinians' living conditions steadily deteriorated. When, in their frustration, the Palestinians periodically fired missiles such as rockets from Gaza into Israel they were met with a disproportionate response of bombing from the Israelis.

Moreover, the blockade has meant that the Palestinians cannot obtain the construction materials needed to rebuild their homes, public buildings and facilities destroyed by Israel. Furthermore, power cuts and fuel shortages have caused hazardous hospital operations, while some Palestinians have resorted to dangerous eating and cooking methods which have resulted in their suffering from serious burns.[6]

The Palestinians cannot escape from Gaza, which in 2010 the British prime minister David Cameron called a 'prison camp'.[7] The Israelis' blockade hems the Palestinians in by land, sea and air.

Thus Israel has imposed a collective punishment on the innocent majority of Palestinians for the sins of a violent few. In Gaza, half of the suffering population are children.

The degradation of the Palestinians

By 2010 there were about 1.5 million Palestinians living in the Gaza Strip (the Israelis having been evacuated in 2005) and about 2 million on the West Bank and in East Jerusalem, together with 400,000 Israelis.[8]

The Palestinians cannot freely leave the Occupied Territories nor move easily between them for work, medical treatment or visiting relatives as they need permits to do so. They have to pass through checkpoints in humiliation and frustration. In addition they can be stopped, searched and arrested at any time.

Furthermore, there is scant work available in the territories and therefore little hope of a prosperous future for the young people. In addition the Palestinians are without adequate medical, educational or social services and sometimes lack even food, clean water and proper sanitation. Israel actually draws off water from Palestinian aquifers beneath Gaza and the West Bank, leaving an inadequate supply for the Arabs.

Indeed in 2012 a UN report said by 2020 Gaza would not be 'liveable': the coastal aquifer, the territory's only source of fresh water, may become unusable by 2016. The report estimates that Gaza's population will rise from 1.6 million to 2.1 million by 2020, when there will not be sufficient schools, houses, hospitals or basic services for them and unemployment levels will soar (from already being 45 per cent).[9]

According to the UN Human Development Index in 2013, Israel's standard of living ranks far higher than that of the Occupied Palestinian Territories: the former is placed high at 16, but the latter as far down as 110. The average life expectancy of the Israelis is 81.9, but that of the Palestinians is only 73. The average years of schooling for the latter is 8, but for the former is 11.9. The average income for the Palestinians is only $3,359 but for the Israelis $26,224.[10]

Conflict 2014

In January 2014, Catholic bishops from North America, Europe and Africa, after visiting Gaza, issued the following statement:

> Gaza is a man-made disaster, a shocking scandal, an injustice that cries out to the human community for a resolution. We call upon political leaders to improve the humanitarian situation for the people of Gaza, assuring access to the basic necessities for a dignified human life, the possibilities for economic development and freedom of movement.[11]

But, in fact, the situation became far worse. On 12 June three Israeli students at 'yeshivas' (religious schools) in the West Bank were kidnapped by

some Palestinians who were not members of Hamas, which was nevertheless blamed for the deaths. Some Israeli extremists promptly kidnapped and
burned alive a Palestinian teenager in revenge, which outraged Palestinians. Meanwhile, Israel, searching for the murderers of the Israelis, arrested
hundreds of Hamas officials in the West Bank and closed their offices. In
Gaza, militants began firing rockets at Israel, which, on 8 July, responded
by launching 'Operation Protective Edge', which involved the disproportionate and indiscriminate shelling of buildings in Gaza, including many
private homes, as the Israeli Defence Force (IDF) claimed that rockets were
being fired from them or kept there. The IDF even, by mistake, shelled six
United Nations Relief and Works Agency shelters, including schools, in vio-
lation of international law and despite the many warnings of UN officials as
to the positions of the UN shelters. On 30 July five Israeli shells hit a school
in the Jabaliya refugee camp, killing fifteen people, mostly children and
women, while they were sleeping and wounding a further hundred people.
The attack provoked international outrage.

The Israelis also blew up the tunnels that the Palestinians used to enter
Israel in order to kidnap Israeli soldiers for bargaining with Israel for the
release of Palestinian prisoners, or in order to attack military targets. As
Hamas's rockets generally missed their targets or were intercepted by
Israel's defence system, the American-funded 'Iron Dome' (only three
civilians in Israel were eventually killed by Hamas's rockets in the whole
of the month-long war), Israel was clearly overreacting but Hamas was
unnecessarily provoking it. Nevertheless Hamas seemed to believe it
helped to keep pressure on Israel to lift the blockade. Hamas said that
it would not agree to a ceasefire unless this were lifted. Despite this not
immediately being achieved, after over three weeks of fighting a ceasefire was negotiated in Cairo on 3 August 2014. This soon broke down
but a further ceasefire was resumed after a few days. By that time nearly
1,900 Palestinians had been killed, mainly civilians, including more than
400 children, while 64 Israeli soldiers had been killed as well as three
civilians in Israel.[12]

After another resumption of hostilities followed by a renewed ceasefire,
brokered again by the Egyptians, the death toll according to the UN had
risen to 2,104 Palestinians killed, including 1,462 civilians, of whom 495
were children and 253 women, while 66 Israeli soldiers, 6 Israeli citizens,
and a Thai national also lost their lives.[13] In addition thousands of houses,
hospitals and clinics were destroyed and thousands of Palestinians made
homeless. The situation was aggravated by the fact that the blockade prevented the necessary construction materials into Gaza.

Israel had alienated much of world opinion by its disproportionate
response to the rocket attacks from Gaza and probably radicalised many

more Palestinians, especially the young, who may well later again use violence against the hated occupier.

Once again Israel had failed to understand that its own security could not be achieved by military force and bloodshed but by negotiating a lasting settlement with the Palestinians.

Pro-Palestinian organisations

As the Palestinians' suffering has remained unrelieved, so have their organisations become more extremist, launching lethal attacks on Israel; yet they would never have been established at all had Israel agreed to the Palestinians' demand for their own state.

In 1964 the Palestine Liberation Organisation (PLO) was formed from the guerrilla groups which had been attacking Israel since its foundation. Dominated by the Al-Fatah group led by Yasser Arafat, the PLO refused to recognise Israel because the latter would not recognise the Palestinians' right to their own state.

After the failure of the Arab states to defeat Israel in 1967, the Palestine Liberation Organisation committed itself to armed struggle, resulting in attacks on Israeli targets throughout the world. Israel's response with revenge assassinations by Mossad only increased Palestinian hostility.

However, in 1988 the PLO officially endorsed the 'two-state' solution and in 1993 recognised Israel's right to exist in peace. In return Israel officially recognised the PLO as the representative of the Palestinian people. But it was too late. In 1979 the Iranian Revolution had taken place, bringing to power an Islamic government that would support financially pro-Palestinian organisations that were more extreme and deadly than the PLO.

The first of these, founded in 1979, was the Palestinian Islamic Jihad, which has carried out suicidal attacks against Israel. The second, founded in 1982, was the much larger Hezbollah. It operates mainly from Lebanon, where it is represented in the Lebanese parliament as it is a social welfare movement as well as a military organisation. It wants the destruction of Israel, on which it periodically launches rocket attacks. It is funded mainly by Iran, Syria and some Lebanese.

The third organisation was Hamas, a Palestinian Sunni Islamic organisation, founded in 1987 by Sheikh Ahmed Yassin. Hamas's charter, drawn up in 1988, declared its goal of destroying Israel and replacing it and the Occupied Territories with an Islamic state. However, this charter was written under the extreme conditions of the 'intifada'. It is debatable whether its leaders all hold these views rigidly still, especially if they were to be involved in Middle East peace talks. Hamas has gained considerable popular support partly because it provides the Palestinians with free medical care, education and social services. Hamas is funded by Palestinian expatriates, private Saudi Arabian and other Arab donors and Iran. In 1993 Hamas began suicide bombing in Israel, making the Israelis even more insecure. In 2006, Hamas won the Palestinian Authority legislative elections. The next year it took power in the Gaza Strip to become a greater menace to Israel than the other pro-Palestinian groups, yet it arose only because Israel had ignored the plight of the Palestinians. I shall consider later the implications of Hamas in power.

Al-Qaeda and ISIS

Mention should be made here of al-Qaeda and ISIS/ISIL/DAESH, which are pro-Palestinian although not founded primarily to liberate the Palestinians. One of the reasons for al-Qaeda's 9/11 attack on the USA was expressly because of the latter's support for Israel to the detriment of the Palestinians' interests.[14] Osama bin Laden's mentor, the Islamic scholar Dr Abdullah Azzam, was a Palestinian seeking justice for his country and motivated by hatred of Israel and its ally the USA. He worked with bin Laden to set up al-Qaeda and probably also helped found Hamas.

ISIS (Islamic State of Iraq and ash-Sham), an extremist offshoot of al-Qaeda, has ambitions to establish a caliphate from Iraq to the Levant. This would include Palestinian territory and as such is yet another example of how Israel will face more and more lethal threats to its existence the longer it denies the Palestinians their own state.

Likud and the power of the ultra-nationalist parties

The third reason for Israel's insecurity is that its policy towards the Palestinians has often been determined by Likud ('Consolidation'), one of the two main Israeli political parties, the other being the Labour Party. Most members of Likud hold that the Occupied Territories were part of Biblical Israel and that the Israelis have a right to build settlements there. This attitude has always been a stumbling block to peace.

In contrast, the Israeli Labour Party has constantly been more open to negotiations with the Palestinians. In 1992 it came to power, led by the courageous Yitzhak Rabin, after Likud had been in government for most of the 1980s.

Greatly helped by skilful Norwegian and American diplomacy, Rabin was willing to negotiate the Oslo Peace Accords, which were signed in the USA by Rabin and Arafat in September 1993. This was the first official agreement between Israel and the PLO and was to be the framework whereby Israel traded 'land for peace'. Israel recognised the PLO as Palestine's official representative; the PLO recognised Israel's right to exist and to renounce violence. Both sides agreed to Palestinian self-rule in Gaza and the Jericho area of the West Bank by 2000. However, tragically in 1995 Rabin was assassinated by a right-wing Israeli extremist and the peace negotiations were halted.

Since then Israel has had only one other Labour government, which was led by Ehud Barak from 1999 to 2001. He offered generous concessions to Arafat. But the latter, probably thinking the new Palestinian state would be divided by Israeli bypass and checkpoints, rejected his offer, especially as the settlement building had continued in the Occupied Territories.

Thus from 1996 until the present (2015) Israel's policy towards the Palestinians has been determined by the hard-line Likud party with the exception of Barak's government and that of Ehud Olmert in 2006. He made a generous offer to the Palestinians, but as he had to resign to face corruption charges for which he was later jailed, nothing came of it.

The Israelis have usually voted for Likud after violent attacks by the Palestinians,[15] as in 1996, 2001 and 2015. But the idea that the use of military force against the Palestinians will give them security is clearly an illusion.

The situation is aggravated by the fact that Likud is usually supported in government by small ultra-nationalist parties that push it to take an even harder line towards the Palestinians. The nationalist parties can and often do impede any peace settlement between Israel and the Palestinians. The Israeli system of proportional representation involves a low electoral threshold which, although raised from 2 per cent to 3.25 per cent in 2014, is still too low. It ensures that the governments in Israel will always consist of coalitions involving the smaller parties which can threaten to bring the government down if their demands are not met. This is at the heart of Israel's problems with the Palestinians and its own security.

No single party has ever won a majority of seats in the Knesset. Therefore the incoming government will offer ministerial posts to members of the smaller parties, who can thus have a disproportionate input when policies are formed. In the Likud government that won the 2009 election, for example, Avigdor Lieberman had considerable influence. He founded and led the Yisrael Beiteinu party, which is supported by Soviet immigrants in Israel and takes a hard line towards the Palestinians. He was both minister of foreign affairs and one of the four deputy prime ministers and thus central to policymaking. During the conflict in Gaza in 2014, Lieberman was pushing Netanyahu to be even harder on the Palestinians, arguing during the ceasefire that Hamas must be defeated, even at the cost of an escalation of the war.[16]

Clearly Israel needs to raise its electoral threshold to limit the power of the smaller parties.

Likud's Ariel Sharon

In 2002 Likud, led by Ariel Sharon, came to power in coalition with ten other parties. Sharon at first seemed a major threat to peace. He had triggered the Second Intifada in 2000 by claiming the Temple Mount complex, containing the al-Aqsa Mosque, would always be controlled by Israel. The Second Intifada then erupted and, unlike the first one, involved suicide bombing attacks on Israel.

In order to stop the violence, the US, EU, UN and Russia had formed themselves into the 'Quartet Powers' and agreed on the 'road map for peace' (a two-state solution) to settle the Israeli-Palestinian problem. However, in 2002 Sharon disrupted the peace process by building a 'separation wall' on the West Bank to prevent Palestinian terrorists from entering Israel. The 'wall' separates some Palestinians from their agricultural land and from the rest of their people on the West Bank.

Then, very surprisingly, in 2005 Ariel Sharon took one of the most courageous and dramatic actions in the whole peace process when he withdrew all the Israeli settlements from the Gaza Strip and four from the West Bank, despite the bitter opposition of his Likud party. Altogether about 8,000 Israelis were forced to leave the Occupied Territories, while Israel remained in control of most of Gaza's land borders, territorial waters and land space. Moreover, there were still nearly 400,000 Israeli settlers living on the West Bank, where two million Palestinians also lived.

Hamas in power, Israel's blockade of Gaza

Unfortunately Israel had left concessions too late. As I explained earlier in this chapter, the Islamic militant Hamas had now developed its electoral strength in Gaza. In 2006 Hamas won the Palestinian Authority legislative elections, refusing to recognise Israel and to eschew violence. At first Hamas and Fatah formed the Palestinian Authority national unity government. But in 2007, claiming Israel and the USA were bolstering Fatah against it, Hamas took control of the Gaza Strip, seized government institutions and replaced Fatah with its own officials.

Israel responded with a land, sea and air blockade of Gaza, allowing only limited humanitarian aid into it. Israel claimed this was necessary to stop Hamas from obtaining more weapons to fire at Israel. Egypt also sealed its border to the Palestinians, who nevertheless dug tunnels to aid the passage of supplies. (After the Arab Spring in 2011, Egypt opened the Rafah border crossing but later closed it again after gunmen attacked border guards.)

Meanwhile the Likud party had split over Sharon's withdrawal from Gaza. Therefore in November 2006 he formed the new Kadima ('Forward') party, which held that both Israel and the Palestinians should have their own state. Unfortunately Sharon had a massive stroke at the end of 2005, from which he did not recover. He was replaced by Ehud Olmert as leader of Kadima, which formed a government in 2006. However, in 2009 Netanyahu became prime minister again and is still in power at the time of writing.

Likud's Netanyahu and the Palestinians 2009–2015

In June 2009 Netanyahu announced for the first time that he would accept a Palestinian state. However, he simultaneously rejected a settlement freeze, which is the main Israeli requirement under the 'road map'. He claimed he had to meet the needs of the 'natural growth' of the population, and thereby showed that peace was unlikely while he was in power.[17]

Since then, Israel's refusal and that of the Quartet (the US, EU, UN and Russia) to attempt to negotiate with Hamas have resulted in more violence. Unfortunately the Quartet has three principles with which a negotiating partner has to comply before joining the Middle East peace talks. They are the recognition of Israel, the renunciation of violence and adherence to previous diplomatic agreements (although most of them were never concluded).

Had it been invited to the negotiations, Hamas might have altered its stance, especially as its charter was written in the extreme conditions of the 'intifada' in 1988. Some of the Hamas leadership might now be prepared to change their positions if asked to the negotiations. The Quartet could have shown greater flexibility and pointed out to Hamas that the principle of recognising Israel is not explicit with regard to borders.[18]

Israel under Netanyahu has blindly continued an oppressive policy towards Hamas, which has only proved counterproductive, culminating in the tragic and unnecessary conflict of the summer of 2014. It was probably this that encouraged Israelis again to elect Benjamin Netanyahu's Likud party to power in 2015, in their mistaken belief that their security demanded a government which would take a hard line with the Palestinians. On the eve of the election, Netanyahu declared that if he were returned to office, he would never establish a Palestinian state.[19] He therefore reversed his endorsement of a two-state which he had made in 2009 in a speech at Bar Ilan University and confirmed many world leaders' doubts that he was ever sincere about peace negotiations.

It is now time to look at the USA's support of Israel, which has undermined its own security and brought down the wrath of Islamic terrorism on its head.

Pro-Israel lobbies in the USA: AIPAC and
J Street –the way to peace?

The fourth source of Israel's insecurity is the support given to it by the USA. This is considerable, mainly because of the strength of the American pro-Israel lobby, especially AIPAC, the American Israel Public Affairs Committee, which is composed mainly of Jews but also of some people who are not, such as Christian Zionists. AIPAC contributes considerably to the campaigning funds of American politicians, both Republican and Democrat, and thus influences Congressional voting.[20]

This lobby is the main reason why the USA pursues a pro-Israel policy and is a major obstacle to peace in the Middle East. Israel would not be able to oppress the Palestinians without American financial, military and diplomatic backing. It is true that an additional reason for the USA's supporting Israel during the Cold War was that it was the only democratic ally of America in the Middle East, but this was not the chief reason then for its support and is certainly not the reason now.

From 1976 to 2004, Israel was the largest annual recipient of US foreign assistance.[21] Owing to the development of Israel's economy, the USA now gives mainly military, not economic, aid to Israel. In 2007, the Bush administration agreed with Israel on a 10-year $30 billion military aid package for the period from 2009 to 2018. During his visit to Israel in March 2013, President Obama promised this would continue subject to the approval of Congress, which later approved $3.1 billion of military financing for Israel for 2014. In addition Israel was to receive another $504 million in funding for research, development and production of Israel's Iron Dome anti-rocket system ($235 million) and of the joint US-Israel missile defence systems David's Sling ($149.7 million), the Arrow improvement program or Arrow11 ($44.3 million) and Arrow111 ($74.7 million).[22] Moreover on 1 August 2014, during the Israel/Hamas conflict in Gaza, the US Senate unanimously passed legislation to provide $225 million in emergency funding for Israel's Iron Dome System, while at the same time some senators criticised Obama for urging restraint on Israel.[23]

American financial and military support for Israel has enabled its governments to resist international pressure to cease building on the West Bank and agree to a Palestinian state. In addition to this aid American citizens are able to send money to Israel through charities and claim tax exemption. They are not allowed to do this for any other country.

However, it has to be said that the more enlightened Jews in the USA believe that Israel's policy towards the Palestinians is both unethical and counterproductive. Some of these Jews have formed J Street to lobby Congress and through the media for a two-state solution to the Israeli-Palestine conflict. They believe that this solution is essential to Israel's survival. To this end they argue that Hamas must be brought into the negotiations. Unfortunately J Street is smaller than AIPAC and needs funds (which could be provided by Arabs as well as Jews desirous of peace).

In addition to financial and military aid, the USA has given Israel unswerving diplomatic support and protection from criticism (including that of possessing an undeclared nuclear weapon).

For over sixty years Israel has denied the Palestinians their own state, dignity and well-being. For the same amount of time Israel has felt very insecure as the Palestinians together with their Arab and Muslim supporters have fought back. The longer Israel ignores the suffering of the Palestinians, the more extreme could be the organisations that arise to attack it and its chief patron, the USA.

Israel's treatment of the Palestinians illustrates the rule of reverse results. However, although peace may now seem a distant prospect, it is still achievable provided Israel and the West realise the need to negotiate with representatives of all the Palestinians. In particular, Israel has to understand that its security lies in withdrawing to the pre-1967 borders after mutually agreed land swaps with the Palestinians, who should have their own state. Jerusalem should be shared and the Palestinian refugees provided with a fair settlement. Only if Israel agrees to this will it have achieved the security which it has denied itself since its foundation. Furthermore the world itself would become a safer place. Those who impress this truth on Israel are its true friends.

Notes

1 Bin Laden quoted by Fred Halliday in *Two Hours that Shook the World* (London 2002), p. 234.
2 Shlaim, Avi, *Israel and Palestine* (London/New York 2010), pp. xiv–v.
3 Shlaim, Avi, *The Iron Wall* (London 2002), pp. 12–16.
4 Morris, Benny, *The Birth of the Palestinian Refugee Problem 1947–9* (Cambridge 1988).
5 Gelvin, James L., *The Israel Palestine Conflict* (Cambridge 2007), pp. 176–9, and Mansfield, Peter, *The Arabs* (London 1988), pp. 288–9.
6 Baroness Morris of Bolton, Hansard, House of Lords, 27 January 2014; Vol. 751, c. 978–80.
7 *The Guardian*, 27 July 2010.
8 PLO Information Politics Dept., London.
9 www.bbc.co.uk/news/world-middle-east-19391809 and http://rt.com/news/gaza-israel-un-report-695.
10 UN Human Development Report 2011 (hdr.undp.org).
11 Sudilovsky, Judith, Bishops Visiting Holy Land Call for Help for "Shocking Scandal" in Gaza, *Catholic News Service*, 16 January 2014.
12 www.bbc.co.uk/news/world-middle-east, 8 August 2014.

13 www.bbc.co.uk/news/world-middle-east-28439404, 1 September 2014.
14 Bin Laden quoted by Halliday, op. cit., p. 234; Gunarartna, Rohan, *Inside Al-Qaeda* (London 2002), p. 5.
15 Prof. Colin Shindler of SOAS, London University, Guest Lecture at University of Notre Dame (London), 1 December 2011.
16 www.the guardian.com/world/2014/aug/13/gaza-conflict.
17 www.aljazeera.com/news, 24 May 2009.
18 www.iss.europa.eu/publications; Goerzig, Carlin, 'Transforming the Quartet Principles: Hamas and the Peace Process', Occasional Paper-No 85, 1 October 2010, p. 25.
19 www.nytimes.com/2015/03/17/world/middleeast/benjamin-netanyahu-campaign.
20 Mearsheimer, John J. and Walt, Stephen M., *The Israel Lobby and US Foreign Policy* (London 2007), pp. 152–3.
21 www.nytimes.com/2015/03/17/world/middleeast/benjamin-netanyahu-campaign.
22 www.crs.gov; Sharp, Jeremy M., Congressional Research Service, US Foreign Aid to Israel, 16 September 2010, Summary.
23 Ibid., 11 April 2014, Summary.

Section 2

Western intervention in Islamic states

2 The USA and Britain helped to bring about the Islamic Revolution in Iran

The last thing the USA and Britain wanted to see in Iran was an Islamic theocracy that funded Muslim fundamentalist movements in other countries. However, this is what they inadvertently helped to achieve by their overthrowing the government in Iran in 1953. Moreover they disrupted Iran's path to democracy, which consequently has never been implemented. The repression of the last shah's autocracy and of the subsequent ayatollahs' theocracy, which has financed violent Muslim extremism abroad, can all be linked to Britain and the USA's interference in Iran. Had Iranian prime minister Mossadeq been able to introduce his reforms in 1953, Iran's subsequent history would have been very different. Although twenty-five years passed before the Iranian Revolution took place and although this outcome was not inevitable, it was made far more likely by the West's earlier body blow to that country's fragile democracy.

Background

In 1901, as a result of the British government's lobbying, the shah of Persia granted an Englishman, William D'Arcy, a sixty-year petroleum and gas concession for the whole of the Persian Empire. D'Arcy, however, initially found no oil and eventually looked for new investors. He found one in the British Admiralty, which wanted to convert British ships from coal to oil to increase the navy's fighting capacity. In 1905 it therefore persuaded the British Burmah Oil Company to invest in D'Arcy's company. Three years later, just before D'Arcy gave up the search for oil, his engineers struck lucky. On the subsequent proceeds, the Anglo-Persian Oil company was formed. In 1914, Britain bought a controlling interest in the company and expanded its cheap oil-fuelled navy, which helped its victory in the First World War.[1] The company later became the Anglo-Iranian Oil Company and eventually British Petroleum. Thus Britain had a vested interest in Persia, which changed its name to Iran in 1935.

During the Second World War the shah decided that his country should remain neutral. But Britain wanted to send trucks of weaponry to the USSR through Iran. The shah refused to allow this. However, the USSR had secured an agreement in 1919 whereby it could send in troops to Persia if it saw a force there that was a threat. It decided to use this right. Therefore in 1941 the USSR and Britain, claiming there were Nazis in Iran, invaded the country and secured the military aid route. The shah then abdicated in favour of his son, Mohammed Reza Pahlavi.

British and American intervention

After the Second World War the foreign troops withdrew from Iran. Meanwhile a nationalist movement developed, wanting to free the Iranian oil industry from Western control. Its leader was an aristocratic politician, Mohammed Mossadeq. In 1951, the shah had to bow to popular pressure and make him his prime minister. At that time the shah had more power than that held by the parliament or 'Majlis'. Mossadeq wished to reverse this situation. Furthermore, although an aristocrat, he carried out important social reforms, freeing peasants from doing forced labour for their landlords and introducing unemployment and sickness benefits for workers.

In order to finance his reforms, with the support of the parliament, Mossadeq nationalised the British-controlled Anglo-Iranian Oil Company. This action moreover was also designed to rid Iran of British influence which was helping the shah retain his power.

Britain responded by launching a campaign for a worldwide boycott of Iranian oil and began covert activities against Mossadeq. In 1952 he broke off diplomatic relations with Britain, which asked the USA to help overthrow him, but President Truman would not support this. However, when President Eisenhower came to power at the beginning of 1953, the new American secretary of state, John Foster Dulles, decided to intervene as he was concerned that Mossadeq was rumoured to be a communist sympathiser. This he certainly was not, although he did work with the Communist Tudeh Party. The USA also wanted to secure a stake in the Iranian oil industry.

Therefore in 1953 the CIA organised a coup against Mossadeq, who foiled it. The shah fled the country. The CIA then bribed mobs to demonstrate against Mossadeq.[2] Concerned that in the turmoil the Communists might take over, the powerful Shia clergy withdrew their support from him. The CIA-backed mobs fought with his supporters, marched on his home and arrested him. He was convicted of treason and sentenced to house arrest for life.

The USA then gained a 40 per cent stake in the Iranian oil industry. The shah was restored and ruled repressively with the help of his sinister secret service, SAVAK. The intervention of Britain and the USA in Iran had stopped its progress towards democracy. Moreover their interference propelled the country towards the Iranian Revolution of 1979 with its export of Islamic extremism.

Owing his throne to the intervention of the USA, the shah remained under its influence throughout his reign. He allowed Western commerce and culture to pervade Iran to the alarm of those opposed to its perceived decadence, especially the clergy and elder members of Iranian society who were concerned with Islamic traditional values. They therefore vigorously responded.

In 1963, clergy in Qom, led by Ayatollah Khomeini, protested moral corruption and the shah's proposed liberal programme. Khomeini was arrested and eventually in 1964 sent into exile. He went first to Turkey, and then Iraq, from where he went to Paris. From there, later on, he recorded sermons criticising the shah's policies and urging him to abdicate. These recordings on cassettes were smuggled into Iran.

Meanwhile other sections of Iranian society, as well as the clergy, became alienated. The villagers had to leave their homes in the countryside and come to work in the towns because of industrialisation and modernisation. They had to spend most of their income on their rents and lacked the support of their community networks.[3] Moreover the gap between the rich and the poor had widened greatly.

Furthermore the middle class were disaffected also as they were not able to have a voice in the running of the country and resented the repression and corrupt government. In addition, the influential bazaar merchants deeply resented the Western banking systems that were being introduced.[4]

The Islamic Revolution

In 1978 after inflation had risen,[5] opposition to the shah became more evident in the form of mass demonstrations and strikes. In September of that year a religious procession turned into mass protest of over a million people against the shah. Martial law was declared and some demonstrators were shot. By December 1978, however, it was obvious that the shah had lost the support of the army as well of the people, who were calling for Ayatollah Khomeini to replace him. In January 1979 the shah left Iran and Khomeini returned to rule Iran the next month, establishing a theocracy.

Since then Iran has been financially supporting Islamic fundamentalist groups outside Iran, such as Hamas and Hezbollah. This is the last thing that Britain and the USA wanted and it probably would not have happened if they had not intervened in Iran in 1953 and overthrown Mossadeq, who was most likely to develop liberal democracy and social justice in the country, because of which he is still highly regarded in Iran. As it was, the shah's repression was followed by even bloodier theocratic oppression when Islamic zealots, probably wrongly thinking they had been given a free hand by Ayatollah Khomeini to deal with the regime's critics, executed thousands of them.

Furthermore, the Iran-Iraq War, which lasted from 1980 to 1988, would probably not have taken place since one of the reasons for it (besides the dispute over the Shatt al-Arab waterway) was the fact that Iran (a Shia Muslim country) was encouraging the Shias in Iraq (the majority) to rise up against the Sunni government of Saddam Hussein.[6] He therefore wanted to overthrow Khomeini's regime and was supported by the West in doing so. Had the Iran-Iraq War not taken place, Saddam Hussein would not have needed to pressure Kuwait to help pay for it nor to invade that country when it refused to get control of the oil wells and much-needed payment. The Gulf War of 1991 then would not have taken place nor that of 2003, to which it eventually led.

The continuing tensions between Iran and the West, with the USA in particular, the domestic repression, above all Iran's support of Islamic extremism abroad, its secretive nuclear activities and growing tension with Israel all probably might never have happened if Britain and the USA had left Mohammed Mossadeq in power in 1953.

The USA and Britain's removal of Mossadeq did not cause the Iranian Revolution but made it more likely. Had he not been ousted the history of Iran would probably have been a dramatically different one of democracy and social stability. As it was the unethical interventions of Britain and the USA in Iran produced results the reverse of those intended.

Notes

1 Mansfield, Peter, *A History of the Middle East* (London 1991), pp. 147–8.
2 Gasiorowski, Mark, 'The 1953 Coup d'Etat in Iran', *International Journal of Middle East Studies*, Vol. 19, No. 3 (Aug 1987), p. 271 et seq.
3 Halliday, Fred and Alavi, Hamza, *State and Ideology in the Middle East* (London 1988), p. 40.
4 Ibid.
5 Ibid.
6 Parsons, Anthony, *From Cold War to Hot Peace* (London 1995), p. 45.

3 Bush and Blair opened Iraq to al-Qaeda and ISIS

The last thing that President George Bush wanted was to open the door to al-Qaeda in Iraq, but this is what he did in 2003 when he invaded that country. The last thing that Prime Minister Blair wanted was to provoke a terrorist attack on Britain, but this is what he did by supporting Bush's invasion of Iraq. Without the vital support of Britain, the USA would probably never have gone ahead with the attack. Had it not done so, ISIS, or the Islamic State, which by 2014 was terrorising the Middle East and horrifying the world, would never have come into existence.

Background

In 1979, Saddam Hussein, as leader of the Baathist party, became the president of Iraq. He was almost immediately plunged into the Iran-Iraq War, which lasted from 1980 to 1988. It began with a dispute over the Shatt-al-Arab waterway that divided the two countries, but was also caused by the fact that theocratic Shia Iran was stirring up the Shia Muslims in Iraq against Saddam's government, which was based on the support of the Sunnis. They, however, made up only about 20 per cent of Iraq's population, centring around Baghdad. Most Iraqis were in fact Shias, while the Kurds were another minority. There was a possibility that Iraq would break up into civil war if Iran were allowed to continue inciting the Iraqi Shias to rebel.

The West supported Saddam with arms sales in the war against Iran, the government of which they hoped would be overthrown. However, it was not. The result was a UN-mediated ceasefire and ultimately an agreement to share the control of the Shatt-al-Arab waterway. Desperate to pay the off the huge debts he had incurred in the war, Saddam asked Kuwait, which had wanted him to defeat Iran, to agree to raise the price of oil, stop producing oil in excess of the OPEC quotas (which lowered the price of oil) and cancel the loan that Iraq had borrowed for the war. But Kuwait refused to do this.

Saddam was angered, particularly as he believed that Kuwait was syphoning off oil from the Iraqi Rumaila oil fields on the border with Kuwait. Further-more, he, like many Iraqis, thought that Kuwait was really part of Iraq and had wrongly been split off from it by Britain in 1922. Other Iraqi leaders indeed had thought the same. (In 1961, the Iraqi leader, Qasim, believing this, had tried to invade Kuwait but was prevented from doing so by British troops.) Moreover, Saddam had wanted to secure a deep water shipping port for Iraq and taking control over the two islands Bubiyan and Warbah would enable him to achieve this.

For these manifold reasons, Saddam Hussein invaded Kuwait on 2 August 1990. Demanding that he withdraw, four days later the UN Security Council imposed sanctions on Iraq. But by the New Year these did not seem to work. On 16 January 1991 an array of coalition forces, led by the USA and Britain, began hostilities, known as 'Operation Desert Storm', against Iraq with an air attack and a ground offensive. By the end of February Saddam had withdrawn his forces from Kuwait.

But the West had not finished with Saddam. After the first Gulf War (as the hostilities were also known), Iraq was still subjected to sanctions which greatly hurt the Iraqi people but not Saddam and his family. A no-fly zone was established and Iraq was subjected to UN weapons inspectors.

President George Bush

On 22 January 2002, in his State of the Union address, President Bush announced that Iraq was part of the 'axis of evil', which, along with North Korea and Iran, threatened the USA's interests. Since 1998 the USA had had a policy of regime change for Iraq after Saddam Hussein had expelled UN weapons inspectors, alleging they were spies.

Between 2002 and early 2003, Bush urged the UN to ensure that Saddam Hussein did not restart a nuclear weapons programme nor possess weap-ons of mass destruction (WMDs), which he was forbidden to do by UN sanctions after the first Gulf War in 1991. Whether Bush's administration manipulated CIA reports to argue that Saddam did have WMDs is still a controversial issue.

In November 2002, under UN Security Council Resolution 1441, Hans Blix and Mohammed ElBaradei led a team of UN weapons inspectors to restart the investigation of the state of Saddam's armaments. By March 2003, Blix had found no stockpiles of weapons of mass destruction and stated that although there was not always immediate Iraqi cooperation the key remaining disarmament tasks would be resolved in a matter of months. Nevertheless the USA tried and failed to get the UN Security Council to pass a resolution to authorise the use of force against Saddam.[1]

Therefore, without UN authorisation, President Bush launched the second Gulf War, 'Operation Iraqi Freedom', on 19 March 2003 against Iraq to destroy the weapons of mass destruction which Saddam was alleged to have possessed and to remove him from power. This action Bush deemed consistent with the policy of the USA to take action against those who 'aided the terrorist attacks' that occurred on 11 September 2001.[2] Yet there was no connection between Saddam Hussein's regime and the 9/11 attack on the USA in 2001. In fact Saddam was strongly opposed to al-Qaeda.

However, it later transpired that the Bush administration had placed much weight on the evidence of a Libyan who was captured in Afghanistan after the fall of the Taliban in 2001, Ibn al-Sheikh al-Libi (or 'al-Libi'). He had been handed over by the CIA for interrogation to the Egyptian authorities who had tortured him. After being beaten and subjected to a 'mock burial', he gave the false information that Iraq had provided training in chemical and biological weapons to al-Qaeda operatives. This claim was repeated by the secretary of state, Colin Powell, in a speech to the UN. Later, embarrassed by the fact the evidence was false, Powell stated that the matter was a blot on his record and that he had not been given all the available intelligence and analysis within the government.[3] Had 'al-Libi' not been brutally tortured, the war in Iraq might not have taken place. This matter shows the great danger of using torture to extract information.

Despite a huge protest by the British people in March 2003, their government, led by Tony Blair, joined the USA's military action against Iraq. Australia and Poland sent much smaller contingents.

By 1 May the war was over. Saddam Hussein was deposed but there were no weapons of mass destruction to be found. The main aims of the second Gulf War were to remove Saddam, which it did, and eradicate weapons of mass destruction, but there were not any to remove. This might have been clearly demonstrated by the weapons inspectors had they been given more time in Iraq.

Nearly 4,500[4] American servicemen lost their lives in the war, and more had been wounded, many maimed. Obviously the USA's coalition partners also suffered losses. Hundreds of thousands of Iraqis were also killed and their country severely damaged. The war cost the USA $806 billion.[5]

Another aim of the war was to take action against those who aided terrorists responsible for the 9/11 attack on the USA. This war objective showed how ill-informed the USA was about Iraq, where there were no members of al-Qaeda ironically until the American invasion. As mentioned earlier, American intelligence had relied on the false information of just one tortured Libyan.

Saddam had, in fact, been keeping al-Qaeda out of Iraq. In 2003, just before the invasion, a Jordanian militant, Abu Musab al-Zarqawi (who had previously ran an Islamic training camp in Afghanistan), had linked up with a Kurdish Islamist militant group in the north of Iraq, Ansar al-Islam. Saddam had viewed this group as a threat to Iraq and had had his intelligence service watching it. Saddam's removal meant that now the organisation was able to establish itself in the country. This it did, aided by the fact that the ill-advised American administrator of the Coalition Provisional Authority, Paul Bremer, foolishly disbanded the Iraqi army, police and intelligence officers, in an attempt to rid Iraq of the influence of the Baathist party. As a result there was not only a breakdown in law and order but also thousands of disaffected soldiers and police looking for employment. This, it seems, they later found with ISIS.

With some of Ansar al-Islam and other Islamic supporters, Zarqawi formed a group, 'Jama'at al-Tawid wal-Jihad' (JTJ), with the aim of forcing the US-led coalition to leave Iraq, where he wanted to establish a pure Islamic state.[6] In 2004 he and his group declared allegiance to al-Qaeda.[7] He contributed greatly to the bloody chaos in Iraq as his tactics were suicide bombings and videoed beheadings. In 2006 he was killed but his al-Qaeda jihadists, who were Sunni, continued their violence.

By 2006, the USA realised that it needed the moderate Sunni tribal leaders to help deal with the Sunni extremists in al-Qaeda. Therefore America paid the sheikhs to unite against al-Qaeda and reduce the violence. This movement, called 'the Sunni Awakening,' was at first successful. However the Shia Iraqi prime minister, Nouri al-Maliki, refused to allow the Sunnis to integrate fully with the Iraqi Security Services or to accommodate them in his administration. Therefore the Sunnis were resentful. When the last American troops had left Iraq in 2011 'the Awakening' had become less effective.

A new dark chapter in the history of al-Qaeda was opening as some of its members in Iraq went to Syria to fight with the rebels, including the al-Nusra Islamists, against Assad's government. In 2013 al-Qaeda in Iraq announced it was allied to al-Nusra. This new group called itself 'Islamic State of Iraq and al-Sham', which is abbreviated to ISIS. ('Al-Sham' is Arabic for Levant and the organisation also called itself ISIL or the Islamic State of Iraq and Levant.) It aimed to turn the whole area into one caliphate, or one Sunni Islamist state, practising Salifiyya jihadism.

The caliph was to be the ISIS leader, Abu Bakr al-Baghdadi, who was born in 1971 and had obtained a PhD in Islamic studies from the Islamic University of Baghdad. It seems that in 2010 he was appointed to the position by a group of former Iraqi intelligence agents, led by Haji Bakr, who had been one of Saddam Hussein's military intelligence chiefs and, according to documents found after he had been killed in Syria, had masterminded ISIS's rise to power.[8] He and the other intelligence officers were Sunnis who had been sacked by Paul Bremer. Indeed the ranks of ISIS were swelled by disaffected Sunni army officers who had likewise lost their jobs and by those Sunnis who believed that the Iraqi government was discriminating against them on behalf of the Shia.[9]

By 2014, ISIS controlled vast swathes of territory in Syria and Iraq amounting to the size of the UK. However, ISIS's methods were so brutal that even al-Qaeda split from it. Nevertheless, some young radicalised Muslims in other countries were attracted to the ideas of ISIS and secretly travelled out to join it.

In Iraq ISIS began calling itself the Islamic State, but many Muslims worldwide condemned it as being non-Islamic because of its brutality, and call it by its loose acronym 'DAESH', meaning 'that which crushes underfoot'. ISIS took to kidnapping foreign hostages and beheading them, showing executions on social media to try to press governments for ransoms or, in 2014, to stop air strikes against it from the West. Here Islamic State may have triggered reverse results to what it wanted, especially by its beheading of the thoroughly decent British aid worker Alan Henning. This shocked the world and increased Western resolve for more military action against it.

Islamic State is financially supported by the oil wells in the north of Iraq that it has captured, as well as support from wealthy donors from Saudi Arabia and Qatar, bank raids and ransom money. In the summer of 2014, ISIS took Mosul with an army a fraction of the size of the defending Iraqi military forces, which fled either because they did not want to kill fellow Sunnis on behalf of the Shia government or because the Iraqi prime minister, Maliki, had replaced the middle-ranking officers with those whom the lower ranks did not trust, or because these had been bribed to flee by ISIS, which raided the banks in Mosul. As ISIS advanced, driving thousands of terrified refugees before it, the USA in August agreed to the Iraqi government's request for military help and bombed ISIS in Northern Iraq, where it was also being attacked by Kurdish forces. The USA's mission was later joined by France, the UK, Australia, Canada, Belgium, the Netherlands and Denmark. (When the USA began bombing ISIS in Syria, it was joined not by Western but by Arab states: Bahrain, Jordan, Saudi Arabia, Qatar and the UAE.) To the dismay of many Americans and British in particular, their countries were yet again involved in military action in Iraq.

The establishment in Iraq of al-Qaeda, its development into ISIS and the USA's further military involvement against it were clearly the opposite of what President Bush had intended. Obviously Prime Minster Maliki must take part of the blame, but had the USA and UK not invaded Iraq in 2003, ISIS would never have existed.

Prime Minister Tony Blair

In his speech to the House of Commons on the eve of the invasion of Iraq, on 18 March 2003, Tony Blair put forward his argument for war:

> Let me tell the House what I know . . . there are some countries, or groups within countries, that are proliferating and trading in weapons of mass destruction . . . there are several countries – mostly dictatorships with highly repressive regimes – that are desperately trying to acquire chemical weapons, biological weapons or, in particular, nuclear weapons capability. Some of those countries are now a short time away from having a serviceable nuclear weapon . . .
>
> . . . terrorist groups in possession of weapons of mass destruction or even of a so-called dirty radiological bomb . . . a real and present danger to Britain and its national security . . .
>
> Of course, Iraq is not the only part of this threat.[10]

In fact Britain was not in danger from an Iraqi attack at that time. Ironically, however, the actual invasion of Iraq by the USA and Britain was probably the most important reason for Britain's being subjected to a terrorist attack on 7 July 2005 that caused fifty-two deaths. In a video that one of the London suicide bombers made to be shown posthumously and was shown on al-Jazeera, Mohammad Sidique Khan said,

> Our religion is Islam . . . Your democratically elected governments continuously perpetuate atrocities against my people all over the world. Until we feel security, you will be our targets. And until you stop the bombing, gassing, imprisonment and torture of my people we will not stop the fight.[11]

Although Khan did not specify Iraq and may also have been referring to Britain's support of the USA's action in Afghanistan and its policy towards Israel to the detriment of the Palestinians' interests, the fact that Britain and the USA had recently invaded and bombed Iraq no doubt played an important part in the terrorist's thinking. Moreover he paid tribute to al-Qaeda leaders, including bin Laden and al-Zarqawi, who was in Iraq. Khan's reference to 'democratically elected' meant that in his view the electorate in democracies could be held responsible for their government's foreign policies in a way that people under dictatorships could not be. However, while he had a point, he had ignored the huge protest of the British public against the war in Iraq and also the great difficulty the public face in influencing the foreign policy of their elected government.

Blair may have sincerely believed Saddam Hussein had weapons of mass destruction, was a cruel dictator and should be removed. But his reasons for supporting the USA's policy could have been more complex: apart from continuing the 'special relationship' he may have felt flattered to work with the American president on the world stage, which would bolster his image and his election chances.

In his autobiography, *A Journey*, Tony Blair states that Britain likes its prime ministers to be recognisable globally:

> I always reckoned that even the ones who didn't like me (quite a few) or who didn't agree with me (a large proportion) still admired the fact that I counted, was a big player, was a world and not just a national leader. It's not a reason for doing anything, by the way, but the British, whatever they say, prefer their prime ministers to stand tall internationally . . . Brits would want to know that in Toulouse people would recognise me . . . It's not the reason for acting in Afghanistan and Iraq or anything else but our alliance with the US gave Britain a huge position.[12]

He records that Robin Cook, who later resigned from his Cabinet position as leader of the House of the Commons because he disagreed with the war, told him, 'it will be a disaster electorally, remember Wilson and Vietnam – he did not side with the US.' But Blair reminded Cook that neither did Wilson win the next election, which seemed to indicate a belief that electoral chances are improved by wars in support of the USA.[13]

In September 2012, in an interview to launch his memoirs, the former UN secretary general Kofi Annan said that Tony Blair could have stopped the war in 2003 had he refused to support the USA without a second UN resolution over Iraq.[14] Why he did not do this can only be surmised. No doubt the USA would not have wanted to invade Iraq without another country's support or the UN's approval.

Whatever Blair's motives may have been, they were certainly clouded by the methods used to persuade Parliament of the need for war against Iraq. In particular, Blair's director of communications, Alastair Campbell, and a Ministry of Defence official, Paul Hamill, prepared a dossier which exaggerated the intelligence findings. In it much was made of a claim that Iraq had weapons of mass destruction that could be activated within 45 minutes. Based on dubious intelligence from a single source passed to an Iraqi exile group in London it seems that the real claim was not about WMD but about battlefield weapons that could be fired at British troops in Cyprus. The dossier used unprocessed intelligence, parts of which were flagged up, and even used material plagiarised from an American-Iraqi student's thesis.[15]

At the Iraq Inquiry in May 2011, Major General Michael Laurie, director general of intelligence collection, stated that the purpose of the dossier was to make a case for war, rather than setting out the available intelligence. This flatly contradicted Alastair Campbell's denial that that was its aim when asked by the Iraq Inquiry.[16]

Tony Blair should have queried the findings in the dossier and had the sources independently investigated in view of his great responsibility as a prime minister about to take his country into a war, with all the bloodshed and suffering that would result. He should also have consulted and listened to far more experts on Iraq, academics and former ambassadors in particular.

Instead Blair seemed to want to believe the evidence, ignored its obvious lack of critical evaluation and wrote a preface to the dossier, highlighting the claim that Iraq could activate weapons of mass destruction within 45 minutes.

It seems that as early as July 2002 Blair privately assured Bush of his support while publicly stating no decision had been taken.[17] However, exactly how and when Blair made commitments to the USA about Britain's military involvement in Iraq may still be kept from the public despite the Iraq Inquiry's request for the release of the correspondence that was communicated using the private channel between the prime minster and the American president at this time. The chairman of the Iraq Inquiry, Sir John Chilcot, requested limited release of the records which the Committee had seen but could not refer to in its report without the permission of Sir Gus O'Donnell, the Cabinet secretary, who refused to allow this.[18]

Besides the huge loss of Iraqi life and that of Coalition partners mentioned earlier, the war also resulted in the loss of 179 British servicemen[19] and many more wounded, and cost Britain £8.2 billion.[20] Blair lost considerable popularity, which was the last thing he wanted to happen. Far from making him stand tall on the world stage, the invasion of Iraq split the Labour Party and alienated Britain's important EU partners, France and Germany. Many British Muslims resented yet another war against those of their faith.

The Iraq War dogged Tony Blair during the election campaign in 2005. The Labour Party did win a third victory, but with the loss of fifty-seven seats. One shock for the party was in the constituency for Bethnal Green and Bow, which has a large Muslim population, where the Labour MP Oona King lost her seat to the Respect candidate George Galloway because of her support for the war. Elsewhere voters who wanted to protest against the war in the election could usually vote only for the Liberal Democrats, who had been against the war but who were unlikely to win the election. (The Conservative Party's leader, Iain Duncan Smith, had actually supported Tony Blair in the war against Iraq.)

Blair's determination to join the American invasion of Iraq seems to have made him unwilling to look at the case for war critically, and to consider giving the weapons inspectors more time in Iraq and other means of dealing with Saddam. These could have included lifting the sanctions against Iraq and encouraging the free flow of trade, business and tourists, which usually opens up a dictatorship, making intelligence gathering and the building up of an opposition movement within the country much easier.

Blair's motives for joining with the USA to invade Iraq seem to have been mixed. He should not have charged into supporting the war, which was without UN approval. He and President Bush enabled al-Qaeda and its spin-off, ISIS, to terrorise the Middle East and radicalise young Muslims around the world, including, to its alarm, the UK. The suicidal bombing in 2005, the beheadings of British aid workers and the death and destruction wreaked by ISIS would not have happened had the West not invaded Iraq in 2003. This action backfired because it was illegal, unethical and precipitate, predictably causing innocent bloodshed without taking due consideration beforehand: another tragic example of the rule of reverse results.

Notes

1 *Christian Science Monitor*, 4 November 2003, www.csmonitor.com/2003/1104/p11s01-legn.html.
2 Letter from President to the Speaker of the House of Representatives, 18 March 2003, http://georgewbush-whitehouse.archives.gov/news/releases/2003/03/print/20030319–1.
3 Finn, Peter, 'Detainee Who Gave False Iraq Data Dies in Prison in Libya', *Washington Post*, 12 May 2009.
4 Casualties in Iraq, Antiwar.com.
5 The Cost of Iraq, Afghanistan, and other Global War on Terror Operations since 9/11. Congressional Research Service, Bellasco, Amy, 29 March 2011. www.crs.gov.
6 Al-Qaeda leaders have proclaimed Iraq a major front in their global terrorist campaign. Office of National Intelligence, 9 July 2005, http://www.dni.gov.
7 Zarqawi pledges allegiance to Osama Dawn, 18 October 2004.
8 *The Times*, 21 April 2015.
9 Caerusassociates.com/news, 23 September 2014, 'Who the US Should Really Hit in ISIS'; see also: www.vox.com/2014/6/20/5824480/why-the-iraqi-army-cant-defeat-isis.
10 Blair, Tony, *A Journey* (London 2010), p. 437.
11 http://news.bbc.co.uk/1/hi/uk/4206800.stm.
12 Blair, op. cit. p. 410.
13 Ibid.

14 *The Guardian*, 29 September 2012.
15 *The Independent*, 22 June 2003.
16 *The Guardian*, 12 May 2011.
17 Ibid., 27 July 2002.
18 *BBC World News*, 18 January 2011, http://www.bbc.co.uk/news/uk-politics-12
210687.
19 Ibid., 21 July 2010, http://www.bbc.co.uk/news/uk-10637526.
20 *Daily Mail*, 21 June 2010.

4   In Afghanistan the USA trained future members of al-Qaeda and American foreign policy backfired

The last thing the USA wanted to do was to arm and train Islamic terrorists in Afghanistan, who would later organise the devastating attack which killed nearly 3,000 American citizens on 11 September 2001. But this is what the USA is most likely to have done, resulting in its involvement in a war that lasted longer than the one in Vietnam. The USA blindly channelled its military and financial support through the Pakistani Intelligence Service, which gave it to the Islamic extremists, as opposed to the moderates, in Afghanistan.

The USA most certainly did not want to lose almost as many American lives in its response to al-Qaeda's attack on the World Trade Center as had been killed in the 9/11 disaster, without destroying al-Qaeda itself. From al-Qaeda's point of view, the last thing that it wanted was to be subject for over ten years to American bombing without forcing the USA to review its policy on Israel. However, this is what both sides incurred by their unethical policies of revenge, which was the motivation for al-Qaeda's 9/11 attack on the USA and for the response of the USA with its 'war on terror'.

The USSR

In 1979 the Communist Afghan government appealed to the USSR for help against the Islamic insurgence (the 'mujahidin') against its rule. The Soviet Union reluctantly agreed and poured in troops to Afghanistan. The USA responded by sending military and financial help to the mujahidin through the CIA and Pakistan's secret service, the ISI.

The USA and the mujahidin

Initially the CIA's covert support for the mujahidin was minimal. However, surprisingly, just two Americans were largely responsible for securing its massive increases: the Texan congressman Charlie Wilson and the Houston socialite Joanne Herring. In 1980, Wilson was able to persuade the House

Appropriations Subcommittee on Defense (which is responsible for funding CIA operations), on which he served, to provide the funds to enable the mujahidin to fight with the most modern weapons instead of their antiquated ones. He had been won over to support their cause by his friend, Joanne Herring. She had visited Afghanistan and had returned with filmed evidence of the severe wounding of the Afghan warriors by the Soviet helicopter gunships.[1]

The USA's support for the mujahidin became part of America's Cold War strategy to stop the spread of Soviet influence in other countries. However, academics, such as Fred Halliday, have commented that it would have been wiser for the USA to have allowed the Communist government in Kabul to have remained in power.[2] Indeed it is unlikely that the 9/11 attack on the USA would have occurred if it had stayed out of Afghanistan. The country might then have remained under the Communist government, which had introduced Western education for girls as well as boys and would have prevented the country from becoming a safe haven for Islamic terrorists. The USA supported the mujahidin only as an anti-Soviet force and not, of course, because it upheld their Muslim beliefs, which were often extreme. Eventually this strategy boomeranged.

The USA's millions of dollars' worth of financial and military aid (involving training as well as weapons, such as Stinger missiles) to the Muslim rebels in Afghanistan went through Pakistan in the form of 'Operation Cyclone', which was partly the result of Charlie Wilson's efforts. The CIA worked closely with Pakistan's secret service, the ISI.[3] Unfortunately, the latter chose to ignore the moderate tribal leaders and to fund radical elements of the mujahidin that were beholden to Islamabad. This was a major error on the part of the CIA, which had not meant, of course, to foster extremists.

From 1979 onwards, Muslim fighters came from all over the world to support the mujahidin, including some Saudis. Among them was Osama bin Laden.

Osama Bin Laden

Osama bin Laden was not on the CIA's radar at this time and was not sought out by the CIA. It is unlikely that he accepted its financial aid as he was a wealthy man. However, he may well have been trained in military and security matters by the CIA, which would also have unwittingly armed and trained other future members of al-Qaeda. Writing in the *Guardian* the day after the London bombings in 2005, Robin Cook, who had been Labour foreign secretary from 1997 to 2001, commented:

> Bin Laden was, though, a product of a monumental miscalculation by western security agencies. Throughout the 80s he was armed by the CIA and funded by the Saudis to wage jihad against the Russian occupation

of Afghanistan. Al-Qaida, literally 'the database', was originally the computer file of the thousands of mujahideen who were recruited and trained with help from the CIA to defeat the Russians. Inexplicably, and with disastrous consequences, it never appears to have occurred to Washington that once Russia was out of the way, Bin Laden's organisation would turn its attention to the West.[4]

In Afghanistan Osama bin Laden came under the influence of Sheikh Dr Abdullah Azzam, who was a Palestinian refugee and a scholar longing to revenge his people's treatment by Israel and the West. He taught in a university in Jordan but was expelled for his extreme views. In 1979 he was again expelled, this time from Saudi Arabia. He then went to teach at the International University of Islamabad.

When the USSR invaded Afghanistan, Azzam issued a 'fatwa' declaring that both the Palestinian and Afghan struggles were 'jihads' in which killing the non-believers in those lands was a moral duty.[5] His jihad doctrine played an important part in the thinking of the mujahidin and of bin Laden's in particular.[6] In 1980 Azzam moved to Peshawar on the Afghan border, where he organised guest houses and training camps to prepare international recruits to fight in Afghanistan. In 1981 Osama bin Laden came to Peshawar. Three years later he and Azzam set up 'Maktab al-Khadamat' to recruit Muslims worldwide to fight in Afghanistan and channel funds and arms to them.

In 1988 the UN secretary general, Javier Perez de Cuellar, negotiated the Soviet withdrawal from Afghanistan. As part of the agreement the USA was supposed to stop arming the mujahidin, but instead it continued to arm the Islamic guerrillas, which led to their victory in 1992.[7]

After the USSR's withdrawal, bin Laden decided to split from Maktab al-Khadamat and establish al-Qaeda or 'database'. He had now come under the influence of an Egyptian doctor, al-Zawahiri, who was also the leader of 'Islamic Jihad'. With the help of this organisation and his own funds, he decided to take the jihad worldwide[8] using his database as a list of potential recruits. In 1996 bin Laden returned to Afghanistan, where the Taliban had come to power, thanks to American aid channelled through Pakistan.[9]

The Taliban or 'students' of Islam were led by Mullah Omar. He believed in a strict interpretation of Islam, including the stoning to death of adulterers and denying education to women, who were forced to cover themselves fully outside their homes. Bin Laden's hatred of the USA's government stemmed mainly from two causes: first the USA's support for Israel at the expense of the Palestinians' interests, and second its presence as an infidel in Saudi Arabia, the land of Mecca and Medina. The first reason for his antipathy probably resulted from the influence of his mentor, the Palestinian Abdullah Azzam.

The attack on the World Trade Center on 11 September 2001

On 11 September 2001 al-Qaeda carried out its devastating attack on the World Trade Center in New York, killing nearly 3,000 people and shocking the world. On 7 October 2001 bin Laden explained his thinking: 'I swear to God that America will not live in peace until peace reigns in Palestine, and before all the army of infidels depart the land of Mohammed. Peace be upon him.'[10]

The USA's foreign policy was, in fact, the reason for the attack. The USA could most certainly have put pressure on Israel to end the suffering of the Palestinians and allow them their own state. It could also have withdrawn troops from Saudi Arabia earlier than when it did do so in 2003. Moreover, as previously pointed out, the USA's financial and military support of the mujahidin in Afghanistan probably resulted in the arming and training of future al-Qaeda members. It also made possible the success of the Islamic rebels and the coming to power of the Taliban, which gave al-Qaeda shelter.

However, in the USA there was much incomprehension as to why their country had been targeted. President Bush did not provide enlightenment when he told the nation, probably with genuine ignorance, 'America was targeted for attack because we're the brightest beacon for freedom and opportunity in the world. And no one will keep that light from shining.'[11] For some reason bin Laden did not broadcast clearly and loudly to the American people what he wanted to achieve. Indeed, his 9/11 attack on their country could be regarded more as an act of revenge rather than an attempt to shock a nation into changing its policies. Probably bin Laden thought the USA understood why its policies antagonised Muslims.

The USA's involvement in Afghanistan clearly had backfired. Had it spent its money earlier on helping the pre-Communist Afghan governments improve the standard of living, education and life chances of their people (which the Communists were at least attempting to do), the USA could have undermined support both for communism and for Islamic extremism.

The USA's response has also partly backfired

After the 9/11 attack the USA wanted to increase its security and to find the perpetrators of the crime. However, instead of issuing international search warrants for its attackers, it launched a massive bombing campaign against Afghanistan. It did not ask itself whether its foreign policy was the cause of the attack (or why Canada, for example, had not been so targeted), and therefore did not change its policy.

In her Reith Lectures, broadcast on 6 September 2011, the former director general of MI5, Eliza Manningham-Buller, remarked on the reaction of herself and her colleagues from MI6 and GCHQ when they had flown to Washington for talks with the CIA the day after the 9/11 attacks. Back in the British Embassy:

> we mulled on the various options open to the US Government and, more widely, to other Western governments. I recall that one of those present argued that the peace process between Israel and the Palestinians needed to be revived, an explicit recognition that the West needed to re-address the open sore in the Middle East that could well have contributed to these events. Those present agreed. It was important, even at this early stage, following a monstrous crime, to consider all possible ways of reducing the likelihood of further attacks.[12]

Unfortunately the USA did not consider the possibility of relieving the suffering of the Palestinians to avoid further attacks on America, but decided on what seems to have been revenge bombing, by launching in October 2001 Operation Enduring Freedom (OEF) with the British Armed Forces and the Afghan Northern Alliance. The objective of OEF was to find bin Laden and other al-Qaeda leaders and bring them to trial, to destroy al-Qaeda and oust the Taliban from power to stop it harbouring al-Qaeda. The OEF, which was not authorised by the UN, was part of President Bush's vaguely named 'war on terror'. The excessive bombing destroyed thousands of lives, wasted billions of dollars and did not destroy al-Qaeda but instead drove Pakistanis to support it.

Of the 'war on terror' Eliza Manningham-Buller made the following insightful comments, which were shared by her colleagues in the British Intelligence Services: 'Despite talk of military action, there was one thing we all agreed on: terrorism is resolved through politics and economics not through arms and intelligence, however important a role these play.'[13] Of the 9/11 attack she observed, 'I call it a crime, not an act of war.'[14] However, the USA was not interested in resolving terrorism through politics and economics. Nor indeed did it consider issuing international search warrants for the perpetrators of the crime of the attack. After a massive bombing campaign the OEF forced the Taliban out of Kabul in a matter of weeks. The Islamic Republic of Afghanistan was set up with an interim government under Hamid Karzai. In December 2001, the International Security Assistance Force (ISAF) was established by the UN Security Council to secure Kabul. NATO assumed control in 2003 of the ISAF, which consisted mainly, though not entirely, of NATO troops.

With regard to Afghanistan's governance, in 2002 Western-backed Hamid Karzai was chosen as the president of Afghanistan's Transitional Administration by the grand assembly of tribal chiefs. In 2004 his government was democratically elected to power by the Afghan people. Women were given more rights and education, but these had not been the aims of the USA's OEF in 2001.

It is true that the coalition forces did oust the Taliban from power and kill some of the leaders of al-Qaeda. But it was not until after ten years of war, in May 2011, that the USA actually found and assassinated Osama bin Laden in his hideaway in Pakistan. Moreover, the USA did not destroy al-Qaeda, which simply operated from other countries. Its spin-off, ISIS, is now terrorising the Middle East.

The war in Afghanistan was not worth the high price paid. By 2014, when most of the international forces left Afghanistan, the war had cost the USA over 2,300 soldiers' lives and the UK 453,[15] and additional lives have been lost by other coalition forces, not to speak of the deaths on the Afghan side and those in Pakistan caused by the drone attacks. The financial costs have been colossal. Precise figures are difficult to obtain, but the Congressional Research Service estimated that the USA had spent about $444 billion on the war by 2011.[16] In 2012 it was reported that the UK had spent an estimated £4 billion a year on the war and probably the total would be about £20 billion at the end of the conflict.[17] The coalition forces have, of course, spent additional sums. The costs of caring for the veterans of the war years after its end would increase the totals.

The enormous sums spent on waging war in Afghanistan could have been better spent on humanitarian projects, such as free health care and education in that country and around the world. This would have won the support of developing countries for the USA and undermined Muslim extremism.

American drones in Pakistan arouse support for the Taliban

Moreover the USA's drone attacks on al-Qaeda or Taliban extremists along the border between northwest Pakistan and Afghanistan have radicalised many Pakistanis and driven them to support the Taliban. As a result Pakistan, already a weak state, is becoming more unstable as extreme Islamism develops in the north and west of the country. Furthermore, the hostility that many Pakistanis feel towards the USA because of its attacks may later bear evil fruit.

America's training of the mujahidin as an anti-Soviet force boomeranged. The 9/11 attack was not made inevitable but probable by the USA's foreign policy. This it should change in its enlightened self-interest. Its decade of bombing Afghanistan and its continuing use of drones in Pakistan could still rebound on the USA unless it contributes generously to the development of these countries. Furthermore it should use its leverage with Israel to insist that the Palestinians are given their own state.

The USA's policy in Afghanistan was as counterproductive as it was immoral.

Notes

1 *The Telegraph*, 2 December 2007, www.telegraph.co.uk.
2 Halliday, Fred, *Two Hours that Shook the World* (London 2002), p. 37.
3 Gunaratna, Rohan, *Inside al-Qaeda* (London 2002), p. 20.
4 Cook, Robin, 'The Struggle against Terrorism Cannot be Won by Military Means', *The Guardian*, 8 July 2005, www.guardian.co.uk.
5 Azzam, Abdullah, 'Defence of the Muslim Lands', www.religioscope.com.
6 Gunaratna, op. cit., p. 18.
7 Halliday, op. cit., p. 38.
8 Corbin, Jane, *Al-Qaeda* (New York 2002), p. 20.
9 Halliday, op. cit., p. 38.
10 Ibid., p. 234.
11 http//archives.cnn.com/2001/US/09/11/bush.speech.text.
12 Manningham-Buller, Eliza, Reith Lectures, 6 September 2011, http://www.bbc.co.uk/reithlectures.
13 Ibid.
14 Ibid.
15 www.icasualties.org/OEF.
16 Bellasco, Amy, 'The Cost of Iraq, Afghanistan, and Other Global War on Terror Operations since 9/11', Congressional Research Service, 29 March 2011, www.crs.gov.
17 *The Telegraph*, 19 May 2012, www.telegraph.co.uk.

5   The West opened Libya to Islamic terrorism

The last thing the USA, Britain and France wanted was to make Libya, an oil-rich country, into a dangerous lawless state teetering on the edge of failure. But this they did when they militarily supported the overthrow of Colonel Gaddafi in Libya in 2011. Their intervention was originally meant to save lives, but their goals soon expanded to include regime change without further reference to the wishes of those UN Security Council members who would have vetoed the intervention had they had they known what the intervening powers would do. The war cost at least 30,000 lives and opened the door to Islamic extremism in Libya, which became almost a failed state through which thousands of migrants flooded into Europe.

Background

In 1969 27-year-old Gaddafi, with fellow officers, overthrew the corrupt king Idris in a bloodless coup and nationalised the oil industry. The West never forgave him for expelling its military and commercial presence in Libya without compensation. He used hard-line tactics with foreign oil companies to quadruple Libya's oil revenues during his first five years in power. With the money Gaddafi established an Islamic welfare state. Indeed he may have done more for the impoverished in his country than many Western leaders have done for theirs. In the words of the distinguished African historian, Ali A. Mazrui,

> The transformation of Libya's social services since the revolution is astonishing. Medicine is free and tuberculosis cases have dropped by more than 80 per cent since 1971. Education is free and compulsory. Between 1969 and 1976 the number of schoolchildren doubled and that of university students quadrupled. Vast construction programmes have rehoused shanty-dwellers in practically free accommodation. There is full employment and comprehensive social security.[1]

Nevertheless, Western media portrayed him as a 'mad dog', sometimes most unfairly. For example, he was once reported as declaring that Shakespeare was an Arab. Journalists had not realised he was a joking, punning on 'sheikh'.[2]

Foreign policy: Libya's/USA's cycle of revenge: Lockerbie

Gaddafi's foreign policy may have been one of the reasons why the NATO powers wanted to overthrow him in 2011. Gaddafi had alienated the West by supporting terrorists whom he regarded as freedom fighters. Thus he helped the IRA with finance and weapons as well as pro-Palestinian groups. From the mid-1980s a lethal cycle of revenge had developed between Libya and the USA, possibly culminating in the tragedy when, in December 1988, a bomb on board Pan Am Flight 103 blew up over Lockerbie, Scotland. All 270 people on board were killed, including 189 Americans. Libya was held responsible for this by the USA, but there is still some debate as to who was really was to blame. If it was indeed Libya it was probably in revenge for the USA's bombing of that country in 1986, killing over 100 Libyans. This, in turn, was in retaliation for Libya's alleged planting of a bomb in a Berlin discotheque, killing three people and injuring seventy-nine American soldiers.

Gaddafi's men may have been operating without authorisation, but eventually, with UN sanctions harming Libya's economy, he allowed two officials to be tried, one of whom was found guilty and imprisoned. Although the Lockerbie issue seemed resolved, there was still residual anger over it in parts of the West.

In 2003 Libya announced that it had abandoned its weapons of mass destruction programme. Gaddafi knew he needed friends in the West to help deal the problem of growing Islamic extremism in Libya, particularly in Benghazi. According to WikiLeaks (publishers of classified files), by 2011 Gaddafi had been supplying the names of hundreds of Islamic extremists in that region to the CIA.[3]

Unrest

In February 2011 unrest broke out in Benghazi. Gaddafi had reason to believe it was stirred up by Islamic extremism. Five years earlier there had been a violent protest concerning some Danish cartoons of the Prophet. Police brutality had resulted in 14 deaths. A 'Day of Rage' on 17 February was organised to commemorate the fifth anniversary of the protest. The organiser was arrested and the mood turned ugly, with crowds demonstrating for better housing, jobs and, inspired by the Arab Spring in Egypt and Tunisia, democracy.

Gaddafi had neglected the people of Benghazi, who belonged to a different tribe than his. Despite this it must be stressed that due to Gaddafi's policies, the UN Human Development Report of 2010 ranked Libya far higher than any other North African state in terms of health, education and income.[4] But Western governments and media, probably ignorant of these facts, portrayed him with contempt.

The demonstrations in Benghazi spread, bolstered by tribal loyalties as well as inspired by the Arab Spring, which was taking place in neighbouring Tunisia and Egypt. Soon more Libyans in the eastern region rose up against Gaddafi's regime. Surprisingly they unfurled flags of the former corrupt king Idris. Some may have been former royalist supporters who had lost their wealth under Gaddafi's socialist reforms. The uprising spread to other cities and the government used heavy weapons to crush it.

The Libyan police were heavy-handed, and violence on both sides increased. The police opened fire, causing fatalities. The mob retaliated by torching police stations.

Then on 22 February Gaddafi made a fatal mistake. In a speech broadcast to the Libyan people about the rebels he declared, 'Get out of your homes, to the streets, secure the streets, take the rats, the greasy rats out of the streets. We are coming tonight . . . Prepare yourselves from tonight. We will find you in your closets.'[5] This was the extreme language of an elderly, eccentric leader who had spoken like this before, so that many Libyans had tended to ignore his speeches.[6] Gaddafi no doubt did think that the 'rats' were al-Qaeda members, as he claimed.[7] Moreover he made it clear that those who laid down their arms would not be harmed. Whatever his intentions, his speech was broadcast outside Libya and caused justifiable alarm that a massacre might take place. Had he not threatened the rebels as he did, thereby giving them the opportunity to secure the West's support, the events that eventually led to his demise might never have happened.

On 26 February 2011, the UN Security Council passed Resolution 1970, demanding an end to the violence in Libya, deciding to refer the matter to the International Criminal Court while imposing an arms embargo on the country as well as a travel ban and an assets freeze on the family of Gaddafi and certain government officials.

National Transitional Council and France

On 27 February the rebels in Benghazi formed the National Transitional Council (NTC) with the aim of overthrowing Gaddafi, claiming that it was the only body legitimately representing the Libyan people.

France was the first country to recognise the NTC. The way in which this happened, leading to its recognition by other Western states which were then involved in removing Gaddafi, was extraordinary. It was seemingly the result of the initiative of just one man: the flamboyant French public intellectual Bernard-Henri Levy. On 23 February he was in Cairo and watched the TV coverage of Gaddafi's threatening speech. Alarmed, he then crossed to eastern Libya, spoke to the rebels, phoned President Sarkozy and suggested that he ought to speak to them. Levy then organised their being flown to France to meet its president. After talking with them Sarkozy decided to recognise their National Transitional Council and summon up international support for it. Whether this was for humanitarian reasons or because appearing as an international statesman would increase his chances of success in the coming French presidential election is difficult to ascertain. Whatever the probably mixed motives, other nations followed France in recognising the NTC. Levy went further, arguing for military intervention in Libya. Knowing that the French foreign minister, Alain Juppe, was opposed to this, he successfully got him excluded from the negotiations, much to the foreign minister's anger.[8]

Sarkozy agreed with Levy, and persuaded the British prime minister, David Cameron, to support a 'no-fly zone' in Libya under the UN auspices. President Obama of the USA was similarly approached but he was more cautious, especially as his armed forces chiefs warned him that a 'no-fly zone' was not necessarily a bloodless option. Nevertheless, he, like the other heads of state, did not want to see Gaddafi carry out a massacre in Benghazi. Obama was finally persuaded to agree to the 'no-fly zone' by three forceful women working for his government: Susan Rice, the USA's ambassador to the UN, Samantha Power, the White House adviser, and Hillary Clinton, the USA secretary of state, who initially disagreed with them and had backed the defence chief Robert Gates's counsel of caution.[9] The Arab League also agreed to support a 'no-fly zone', which meant that intervention in Libya could not been seen as a purely Western action.

No-fly zone

Therefore, on the night of 17 March 2011, the Security Council approved UN Resolution 1973, with five members abstaining and ten in favour. It set up a 'no-fly zone' over Libya, imposing a ban on all flights in the country's airspace. It further demanded an immediate ceasefire in Libya, an end to attacks on civilians and the tightening of sanctions against Gaddafi's regime and its supporters. The Security Council authorised member states, acting nationally or through regional organisations or arrangements, to take all necessary measures to protect civilians under threat of attack in the country, including Benghazi, while excluding any form of foreign occupation force on any part of Libyan territory. Member states were requested immediately to inform the Secretary General of such intended actions.

It was the phrase 'all necessary measures to protect civilians' that was later extended by the USA, France and Britain to mean regime change. Russia and China would no doubt have used their veto had they known what was to happen. As it was they abstained, as did Brazil, India and Germany.

On March 19 a multi-state coalition began a military intervention in Libya to implement the UN Resolution 1973 and established a naval blockade. Without waiting to see if Gaddafi accepted the no-fly zone, the US launched missiles against Libya's air defences, Britain and France undertook sorties across Libya and the latter carried out airstrikes against Libya's tanks. Libya's army had meanwhile been regaining control of Benghazi, where armed militia (some of them Islamist) had emerged, but the army had to withdraw after the airstrikes. The attack against the Libyan forces was initially led by France and Britain with command shared by the USA. President Obama clearly did not want the USA to take the lead role.

NATO and regime change

On 31 March NATO took charge of the Libya mission and militarily supported the rebels, although many commentators in the West as well as elsewhere did not think this was authorised by UN Resolution 1973. In Britain, the respected peace negotiator Lord Alderdyce warned, 'It should not be that we are backing the rebels against Colonel Gaddafi but that we are backing international law for the protection of all of the citizens of Libya, of whichever side, and much beyond.'[10] He was supported by others in the House of Lords, including the distinguished lawyer Baroness Kennedy:

> We are now falling into the same trap as we did in Iraq, where we are over-reading resolutions 1970 and 1973 in order to justify what was not within the ambit of those who voted in favour of them. Resolution 1970 made it clear that there was a total embargo on providing arms to either side. Resolution 1973 did not vary that position. It said that 'all necessary means' should be used to prevent a massacre, but that is not the same as providing arms to the rebels. Neither is it about regime change.[11]

In Russia, Prime Minister Putin deplored the use of force, stating that the UN resolution was 'surely flawed and lame . . . as it allows intervention in a sovereign country'.[12]

Meanwhile the African Union put forward a peace plan to which Gaddafi agreed. Its main points were an immediate ceasefire, the unhindered delivery of humanitarian aid, protection of foreign nationals, a dialogue between the government and rebels on a political settlement, and the suspension of NATO airstrikes. But the rebels in Benghazi rejected it because it did not demand Gaddafi's exit from the government. NATO powers did not try to persuade them to accept the peace plan; rather it took their side against Gaddafi.

In the Western mass media Gaddafi was demonised. There was no appreciation of any good that he had done for Libya. In October 2011, the military support of NATO enabled the rebels to overthrow Gaddafi's regime. They could not have done this without such backing; all in all NATO flew over 26,000 sorties. One of them bombed Gaddafi's convoy as he was leaving his home town of Sirte. Gaddafi was captured by the rebels, humiliated and shot.

Regime change had been achieved but at a very high price and was unethical, without the approval of Russia, China, Germany, India and Brazil in the UN Security Council. It was an ill-informed intervention without any comprehension of the problems Gaddafi was facing with regard to the Islamic extremists. Moreover, having ousted him, the West had no plans to reconstruct the country.

The objective of NATO's intervention in Libya was supposed to protect the lives of civilians. But in September 2011 the interim health minister in Libya announced that at least 30,000 people had been killed in the civil war, and over 50,000 had been wounded, while 4,000 were still missing. He expected the final figure for the dead to be higher.[13] Libya's population is just over 6 million. Besides the high death toll, much of Libya's infrastructure has been destroyed, while thousands of migrant workers have been displaced.

Moreover, Islamic extremism, which Gaddafi was trying to combat in Libya, has continued to spread. In September 2012, Islamists in Benghazi killed the American ambassador Christopher Stevens, and three other diplomats from the USA. NATO's intervention has helped the spread of Islamism in Libya. This is the last thing that the West wanted for that oil-rich region so near to the West. In addition there was a proliferation of thousands of armed militia, lawlessness, continual car bombings and other forms of violence accompanied by a breakdown of normal governmental life, which prompted comments that Libya, in 2015, was a failed state.

The Syrian conflict: The UNSC paralysed after Libya regime change

Furthermore, as an even greater disaster unfolds in Syria, the UN Security Council (UNSC) has been unable to intervene because of what Russia and China regard as the West's betrayal in Libya.[14] Russia and China had not intended that their abstentions over UN Resolution 1973 should allow regime change. Therefore unsurprisingly, they are not co-operating on the UNSC with the West in ending the civil war in Syria, especially as both the USA and the UK have called for an end to the government of President Assad of Syria, raising the issue of whether a no-fly zone would again mean regime change.

Further fallout: Migrants to Europe, Tuareg fighters to Africa

In addition, by 2015, thousands of migrants from countries of conflict and poverty were pouring over Libya's undefended borders and smuggled by people traffickers into unsafe ships destined for Europe. As a result, hundreds have been drowned while Italy and Greece have been overwhelmed by the migrants, who pose a huge problem for the EU to solve.

The overthrow of Gaddafi has also meant that thousands of Tuareg fighters (nomadic Berbers), whom Libya had been recruiting since the 1990s, returned home to Mali with their weapons. This resulted in an Islamic takeover of the north of that country. The West's intervention destabilised the area, which became awash with weapons. The effects on the sub-Sahara of the fall of Gaddafi were probably not considered by the Western powers before they intervened and were certainly not what they had wanted.[15]

The NATO powers' intervention caused a huge loss of life, which was the opposite of their expressed aim. In addition they opened Libya to Islamic terrorism, reduced the oil-rich country to a parlous state, destabilised the regions around it and caused paralysis in the UN Security Council. These were the unwanted and unintended consequences of the overthrow of Gaddafi, which was illegal as well as unethical.

Notes

 1 Mazrui, A.A. and Tidy, M., *Nationalism and New States in Africa* (Heinemann, 1989), p. 267.
 2 *The Times*, 4 August 1989, 2a.
 3 Ibid., 22 March 2011.
 4 UN Human Development Report 2010, hdr.undp.org.
 5 http://mydd.com/users/inoljt/posts/gaddafis-fateful-speech. Politikalblog:http://thepolitikalblog.wordpress.com/2011/12/9/gaddafis-fateful-speech.
 6 Ibid.
 7 *The Times*, 22 March 2011.
 8 http://www.lexpress.fr/actualite/politique/bhl-assassine-juppe.
 9 www.nytimes.com/2011/03/19/world/africa.
10 Hansard, 1 Apr 2011, Column 1472, www.publications.parliament.uk/pa/ld201011/ldhansrd/text/110401–0001.htm.

11 Ibid.
12 'Countries Slam Western Air Raids against Libya', *People's Daily*, Online, 22 March 2011, http://english.people.com.cn/90001/90777/90855/7327318.html.
13 *Huffington Post*, 8 September 2011, www.huffingtonpost.com/20111/09/08/libya-war-died_n_953456.html.
14 Kramarenko, Alexander, Minister Counsellor of the Embassy of Russia to Great Britain, Lecture to the Great Britain-Russia Society, 30 October 2013.
15 Melly, Paul, 'Gaddafi's Guns Trigger Collapse', *The World Today*, Vol. 68, No. 11.

Section 3

China and Russia

6   Mao turned China capitalist

The last thing that Mao wanted for China was its return to capitalism, but his extreme socialist policies resulted in this happening.

The Communists' reforms

When the Communists came to power in China in 1949 they restored peace and stability to the war-torn country by establishing a dictatorship aimed at ending the poverty and exploitation of the majority of people. To this end, capitalism was abolished and socialism implemented. All workers, whether in the towns or countryside, were attached to work units or 'dan-hui', which provided them with secure employment, free health care, cheap housing, pensions and childcare. This radical form of social security was known as the 'iron rice bowl'. Education was free up to university graduation. In addition women were liberated from such practices as forced marriages and had the same educational and employment rights as men.[1]

Through the Communists' reforms the majority of Chinese were given more enjoyable, longer lives and life chances of which they had previously never dreamed. This achievement was the more dramatic as China's population was, as it is now, the largest on earth. No other political party in the world has achieved so much for so many of its poor in such a short time. The impoverished masses in India by contrast remained illiterate and in poor health, despite its government being democratically elected.

Mao's Hundred Flowers Campaign resulted in criticisms of the Communist system and the consequent Anti-rightist Campaign

As in other Communist countries during the Cold War, there was the constant fear that those who had lost their wealth in the revolution would try to overthrow the government with Western help. Therefore the Communists suppressed any hint of 'rightist' thinking, using violence against suspected 'counter-revolutionaries'.

In 1956, Mao launched his Hundred Flowers Campaign, named after an ancient saying, 'Let a hundred flowers bloom, let a hundred schools of thought contend,' in which he encouraged intellectuals to express themselves freely about the reforms. Why he did this is not clear, but he may have wanted to humble Communist officials who had become arrogant or to lure out the Party's enemies. He may also have expected praise for the Party's reforms. Indeed it could be that he had introduced free speech too early.

Whatever the reason, Mao was angered when in the spring of 1957, the intellectuals, who were mainly from the upper classes, criticised the whole Communist system. He therefore launched the Anti-Rightist Campaign and had the critics labelled as 'rightists'. Many of them lost their jobs and were sent to the countryside. As a result, two years later, when it was clear the Great Leap was going wrong, the intellectuals did not dare to criticise it openly. Nor were there the statisticians and economists available for their guidance as many had been sacked in the Anti-Rightist Campaign. It is now time to look at the Great Leap.

The Great Leap Forward (1958–60) resulted in possibly 30 million deaths and Mao's demise from power

In 1958, Mao moved to extreme socialism, launching the Great Leap Forward as the next step to communism. He and other Communist leaders hoped thereby to maximise the productivity of the masses and transform China's agrarian economy into a modern, but communist, industrial one.

The Communists, having freed the peasants from landlord exploitation, had gradually grouped them into co-operatives, and then collective farms. In the Great Leap, the peasants were forced into enormous communes, where they were obliged to live communally, giving up family life. They did not want to live and work this way and had no incentive to increase their productivity.

Moreover a severe drought occurred when the communes were established, resulting in low grain yields. But the officials in charge falsified the statistics of the harvests out of fear that they would be criticised for incompetence. They took what grain was produced, including that which the peasants needed for food, and sent it to the cities. As a result the peasants began starving to death. During the Great Leap possibly as many as 30 million peasants died.[2] It is difficult to ascertain the exact number as statistics for this period are unreliable. Furthermore, it is impossible to know whether the peasants would have died even if the Great Leap had not been implemented since it coincided with a severe drought. Natural disasters used to kill millions in China where governments prior to the Communists did very little to help them. It was in fact the Communists who first established governmental policies of saving and protecting the Chinese from drought and floods. The Great Leap was not Mao's responsibility alone, since the other leaders supported or did not object to it. Moreover, the officials involved in the grain production of the communes did not inform the leadership that the Leap was going wrong for fear of losing their jobs. Had Mao not launched the Anti-Rightist movement, or the Hundred Flowers Campaign that preceded it, the officials may have been more forthcoming with their knowledge. The errors of judgement resulted in the deaths of millions. But this was not the intention of Mao nor the other Communist leaders. He cannot be portrayed as a mass murderer as some Westerners have tried to label him. He did not want the peasants to die but rather to live better, as his reforms show. There is a great difference between unintentionally causing deaths and deliberate murder.[3]

Mao also urged the Chinese to build furnaces in their backyards and make steel by melting down kitchen utensils and garden tools. The steel was useless. He had vainly hoped by this method of steel production that China would catch up with the West industrially within fifteen years.

Not all the Chinese leaders were unaware of the disaster that was unfolding. In 1959, one of the veteran Chinese leaders, Marshall Peng Dehuai, went to see Mao to tell him the Great Leap was not working. But Mao responded by dismissing him, replacing him with Lin Biao as minister of defence.

By this time Mao should have heeded the warnings that the Great Leap had failed, but instead he tried to persist with the policy. This was too much for the other Communist leaders, who in 1960 forced Mao to give up running the economy. He handed over the position of the chief of state to Liu Shaoqi, who with Deng Xiaoping, the Chinese Communist Party's secretary general, set about dismantling the communes and giving the peasants financial incentives instead. Liu and Deng had become convinced by the failure of Mao's extreme socialism that the way forward was more economic freedom: to allow the peasants to have their own private plots and sell part of their produce at rural markets on a private basis. This was an important step in the opening of China's economy.

The Cultural Revolution (1966–76) was a decade of chaos that undermined belief in Mao's policies

Mao deeply resented his loss of power and also believed that Liu Shaoqi was putting China on a capitalist road. However, most of the Communist Party leaders supported Liu. Therefore, to regain control of policy, in 1966 Mao launched the 'Great Chinese Proletarian Cultural Revolution', based on the

Chinese young people, who were urged to eradicate 'bourgeois influences' wherever they found them, including people senior to them, especially university staff. In this revolution Mao was supported by the 'Gang of Four', which included his wife, Jiang Qing, and three other rapidly promoted Communists.

Groups of students organised themselves into 'Red Guards', which first carried out big poster criticisms of university staff, and then dragged them out to 'struggle sessions', denouncing and humiliating them, at times forcing them to kneel on broken glass or stand in 'airplane' position with arms outstretched while they were 'struggled against'. Sometimes they were beaten to death. Their 'bourgeois' paintings, books, antiques and any Western possessions were destroyed. Lecturers were forced to attend struggle sessions daily. Some committed suicide.

Intellectuals in every profession were vilified as 'stinking number nine' and sent to the countryside every six months to learn from the peasants. As a result the economy was in chaos as there was no one of ability to run it, although Zhou Enlai, the brilliant prime minister, managed to keep the administration running. Why he did not oppose Mao's policies remains a mystery, although he obviously was concerned with self-preservation.

The Red Guards were given free transport to go throughout China, criticising 'bourgeois' attitudes. Parading people publicly in dunce caps was one of their favourite methods. Soon most of China was precipitated into the turmoil of public criticisms, beatings, looting, smashing and killings. The Communist Party was torn apart by warring factions and power struggles.

Mao himself would make appearances in Tiananmen Square, adulated like a pop star by the Chinese young people, who would wave the Little Red Book of his thoughts. Meanwhile, Liu Shaoqi was 'struggled against', sent to detention camp and although ill was denied medical treatment. He died alone in a barn.

Millions of people were harmed by the chaos of the Cultural Revolution, which did not end until Mao died in 1976 and the Gang of Four were arrested. Whether Mao had become ill and given to grandiose ideas or whether he was in full control of his faculties may never be known. Certainly his thought processes seemed very different from those he had shown decades earlier as a young revolutionary, when he wrote his careful analysis on the Hunan peasant movement or with great sensitivity on the suicide of Miss Chao, who took her life rather than face a forced marriage.[4]

Break up of central planning system

However, what was important for China's future economic development was that unwittingly, through his Cultural Revolution, Mao had disabled the Chinese Communist Party's central planning control of the economy, which would have prevented capitalism from being later being implemented.

Decision making had become decentralised, and thus China was more ready than the USSR to throw off the Stalinist model of central planning.[5]

Inevitably local economic initiatives developed, which were later built upon. One of the most important of these was the beginnings of the 'household responsibility system', begun by some peasants in a village in Anhui. They persuaded the local cadres to allow the peasants to be responsible for the production and management of their farms.

Moreover, Mao's extremism had caused such suffering that it had resulted in the last thing he had wanted: the rejection of his ideas.

Deng Xiaoping came to power in 1978, reversed Maoism and introduced economic reforms which turned China's economy capitalist

After Mao's death, Deng Xiaoping emerged to the fore of the CCP. He had suffered considerably during the Cultural Revolution when he was purged from the party and sent to the countryside. His son had been pushed from a window by Red Guards and permanently crippled. Deng was rehabilitated in 1973, and then accused of encouraging mass demonstrations when Zhou Enlai died. In 1976 he was purged again. In 1977 he was rehabilitated for a second time. He was determined to reverse Mao's radical socialist policies.

At the end of 1978 Deng Xiaoping and other moderates gained the upper hand at the Third Plenum of the Eleventh Central Committee of the CCP, which adopted their policies of the four modernisations (in agriculture, industry, science and technology and defence) as Party policy. It had been Zhou Enlai who had first raised the matter of the four modernisations in 1965 but the Cultural Revolution had made it impossible. Deng had raised them in 1975 but was purged in 1976. Now he was determined to implement them. He made it clear that the Third Plenum's decision to concentrate on modernising the country and not on class struggle was due to the negative experience of the Cultural Revolution:

> Our successes have provided us with valuable experience, and so have our mistakes. Although we thoroughly condemn the 'cultural revolution', we recognize that it was useful to the extent that it taught us a lesson . . . (The Plenum's) policy decision won universal support from Party members and the people. Why? Because we had before us the alternative example of the 'cultural revolution'. So the 'cultural revolution' has turned out to be valuable.[6]

A key idea of the reforms was shifting power and responsibility away from centralised control on to individuals, so that in agriculture the 'household responsibility system', mentioned earlier, was adopted in most rural areas. As peasants were allowed to grow and sell food privately, many of them soon grew rich. In industry individuals were first allowed to employ up to seven workers but soon new businesses were springing up.

In 1979 Deng established four Economic Zones, which were tax holidays for foreign investors (similar to those in Taiwan). The zones were Shenzhen, just north of Hong Kong, Shantou and Xiamen opposite Taiwan, and Zhuhai near Macao. Later Shanghai and other ports were opened up. In 1980 China entered the International Monetary Fund and the World Bank. During the 1980s China introduced trademark, patent and inheritance laws and in 1994 a bankruptcy law was implemented.

Gradually, and then with astonishing speed, China's economic development took off, as the Chinese, aided by foreign investment and expertise, revealed colossal entrepreneurial energy. The standard of living of the Chinese rose dramatically and millions were lifted out of poverty. By the 1990s China's economic growth rate was reaching double digits. However, this was at the expense of the breaking of the iron rice bowl, the ending of job security and even free health care and university education.

Ending collectivisation, central control and egalitarianism, introducing free market principles and allowing individuals to follow their own economic interests and choose their own jobs meant the end of Mao's method of economic development. Mao's later policies of the Great Leap and of the Cultural Revolution had resulted in Deng and his supporters being determined to jettison his ideas.

In 1980, talking to leading comrades of the Central Committee, which was appraising Mao, Deng commented: 'Generally speaking, Comrade Mao Zedong's leadership was correct before 1957, but he made more and more mistakes after the anti-Rightists struggle of that year.'[7] Deng was a severe critic of the fact that Mao's later policies had impoverished China. In 1985 he remarked,

> Our experience in the 20 years from 1958 to 1978 teaches us that poverty is not socialism, that socialism means eliminating poverty. Unless you are developing the productive forces and raising people's living standards, you cannot say you are building socialism.[8]

Deng's well-known emphasis on the merits of getting rich was in reaction to Mao's later policies:

> During the 'cultural revolution' there was a view that poor communism was preferable to rich capitalism. After I resumed office in the central

leadership in 1974 and 1975, I criticised that view. Because I did so, I was brought down again. There can be no communism with pauperism, or socialism with pauperism. So to get rich is no sin. . . . To get rich in a socialist society means prosperity for the entire people.[9]

Deng argued that the Cultural Revolution was a bad thing that turned into a good thing since it provided lessons to draw on:

> Thus bad things can be turned into good things. It is because we reviewed our experiences and drew the lessons of the 'cultural revolution' that in the late 1970s and early 1980s we were able to formulate the policies that are now in force.[10]

Mao's mistakes were so considerable that they resulted in the abandonment of his socialist policies and the introduction of capitalism, which no doubt would have been strongly resisted by the CCP had he not implemented such extreme ideas after 1957. The Party did not say it was introducing capitalism, calling its reforms 'socialism with Chinese characteristics'. In 1992, when touring southern China, Deng said that the market economy also happens under socialism, which does not necessarily mean state planning. But by the end of the 1990s China's economy seemed more capitalist than that in many Western European social democracies. China's economy is now ninety times larger than in 1978, when Deng Xiaoping introduced the limited free market reforms, and has been growing at the rate of 10 per cent a year. By mid-2010 it became the world's second largest economy, after the USA, pushing Japan to third place. The achievement of the Chinese is truly remarkable – and it might never have happened had Mao not inadvertently discredited collectivism and central planning by his extremism.

Notes

1 For studies on the Chinese Communists in power see: Meisner, Maurice, *Mao's China and After* (New York 1999); Schram, Stuart R., *Mao Tse-tung* (Harmondsworth, England 1970); Spence, Jonathan, *The Search for Modern China* (New York 1999); Macfarquhar, Roderick and Fairbank, John (eds), *Cambridge History of China*, Vols 14–15 (Cambridge 1995). For a study of the violence involved, see Dikotter, Frank, *The Tragedy of Liberation* (London 2013).
2 Meisner, op. cit., p. 237.
3 Ibid., p. 237, for an interesting discussion of this point.
4 Schram, Stuart R., 'Miss Chao's Suicide' in *The Political Thought of Mao Tse-tung* (Harmondsworth, England 1969), pp. 334–7.
5 Shirk, Susan L., *The Political Logic of Economic Reform in China* (Berkeley 1993), p. 13.

6 Deng, Xiaoping, *Selected Works of Deng Xiaoping (1982–1992)*, Vol. 3 (Beijing 1994), p. 267.
7 Deng, Xiaoping, *Selected Works of Deng Xiaoping (1975–1982)*, Vol. 2 (Beijing 1984), p. 280.
8 Deng, Xiaoping, *Selected Works of Deng Xiaoping (1982–1992)*, Vol. 3 (Beijing 1994), p. 122.
9 Ibid., p. 174.
10 Ibid., p. 175.

7 Stalin caused the collapse of the Soviet Union

The last thing that Stalin wanted to do was to set the USSR on the path to eventual financial ruin, but this is what he did when he enforced the collectivisation of agriculture in the 1930s and took control of Eastern Europe after 1945. Neither of these harsh policies was essential to the implementation of Soviet Communism, and ultimately they played an important part in its collapse.

Soviet Communism

The Bolshevik Revolution in 1917 gave workers throughout the world confidence that life could be better for them, seeming to offer a real example of what could be done for the poor. Indeed the revolution raised questions internationally as to whether all governments should not be concerned with public welfare. The USSR provided its citizens with full employment (though with over-manning) and no inflation. This was in sharp contrast with the West in the 1930s, where the Great Depression resulted in mass unemployment and hunger marches. In addition Soviet citizens received outstanding benefits in the form of free education up to and including the university level, a free health service, including recuperation in state convalescent homes, free childcare, cheap housing and old-age pensions. Moreover Soviet scientists were directed to find cures for diseases and these cures were made available to all.

The Bolshevik Revolution was the spark that eventually ignited revolutions internationally from China to Cuba, lifting millions of people out of poverty and thus transforming their lives. And everywhere that communism went, so did the beauty of the Russian ballet, available for everyone to see cheaply and for their children's training as dancers.

However, there was a darker side to the Soviet Union. Lenin was no angel, but his successor, Stalin, was so controlling and brutal that much of the idealism of communism was destroyed. Its positive features were compromised as he terrorised the USSR in the 1930s with purges and show trials, executing thousands and sending millions to the Gulag prison camps. This persecution had nothing to do with communism but was the result of Stalin's paranoia and some Russian traditional oppressive political practices. The poet Anna Akhmatova described the terror thus:

> Stars of death stood over us
> As innocent Russia squirmed
> Under the blood-spattered boots and tyres
> Of the black marias.[1]

Nevertheless, it was Stalin's mighty will that pulled Russia into the twentieth century. His Five-Year Plans turned the USSR, where the state owned all businesses and factories, into an industrial power by the time of the outbreak of the Second World War. This was no mean feat.

Forced collectivisation of agriculture

Unfortunately, Stalin also insisted on the forced collectivisation of agriculture, whereby the peasants had to give up their land to work on huge state farms. This was a disastrous policy for the USSR and a major cause, together with Stalin's control of Eastern Europe, of the eventual collapse of the Soviet Union.

Stalin thought that the large state farms would be very efficient as large machinery could be used on them. Any excess peasants would become workers in the towns. He wanted to introduce this policy because food shortages had occurred in the late 1920s. The matter was debated in the Politburo in 1928–29 and opposed by Alexei Rykov and Nicolai Bukharin. They had seen that agriculture had flourished when the peasants had been given back their land to farm under Lenin's New Economic Policy. This had replaced his War Communism in 1921.

At the end of the decade Stalin nevertheless insisted on enforced collectivisation. When this was strongly resisted by the rich peasants or 'kulaks', he sent in the army to crush them by executions or by deportation to the labour camps. About five million kulaks died. To protest at the policy they had burned their crops and slaughtered their animals. This led to a great famine in Ukraine, where possibly ten million people starved to death. Nevertheless, Russia later became self-sufficient in grain and began to export it by the end of the 1930s. However, the grain yield did not reach the high levels that Russia had met before the First World War, when it was the breadbasket of the world.

Stalin's policy of collectivised agriculture was continued after his death in 1953. By the 1960s the USSR was becoming alarmed that its grain output was steady but its population was rising. In 1963 Khrushchev informed the leaders of the Socialist bloc that the USSR would no longer be able to supply them with grain. In that year the Soviet state used a third of its gold reserves to buy millions of tons of grain. Khrushchev commented, 'Soviet power cannot tolerate any more the shame that we had to endure.'[2]

The Soviet Empire in Eastern Europe and the Cold War

The second policy of Stalin that led to the financial ruin of the USSR was the establishment of the Soviet Empire in Eastern Europe. This played a major part in the Cold War and led to the USSR spending far more than it could afford on armaments.

In 1946 Winston Churchill declared in his famous speech at Fulton, Missouri, in the USA that

> Nobody knows what Soviet Russia and its Communist international organization intends to do in the immediate future, or what are the limits, if any, to their expansive and proselytizing tendencies . . .
>
> From Stettin in the Baltic to Trieste in the Adriatic an 'iron curtain' has descended across the Continent. Behind that line lie all the capitals of the ancient states of Central and Eastern Europe, Warsaw, Berlin, Prague, Vienna, Budapest, Belgrade, Bucharest and Sofia, all these famous cities and the populations around them lie in what I must call the Soviet sphere.[3]

In fact Churchill played a part in bringing down the Iron Curtain himself as he had ignored Stalin's requests during the Second World War that the Western Allies open a Second Front in Europe, taking some of the Nazi onslaught off the Soviet Union. Churchill had thereby greatly increased Stalin's distrust of the Western Allies. Furthermore, during the 1930s, the Soviet leader had been rebuffed in his attempts to get Britain and France to join him in a popular front against Nazism. Moreover, he was well aware that the West had sent considerable military support to the White Russians to overthrow the Bolsheviks during the civil war during 1918–21. He was further alienated by the fact that his Western Allies did not share with him the secrets of their A-bomb, which the USA had used in 1945, partly to thwart the USSR's planned invasion of Japan. As a result, after the Second World War Stalin left the Red troops in Eastern Europe, where he created a ring of buffer states to prevent the USSR ever again being attacked from the West. However, although he thought the Iron Curtain was a strong defence, it actually caused much alarm in the West and was a major cause of the Cold War, which drained the USSR's coffers.

There has been considerable debate as to the causes of the Cold War, which cannot be fully explored here, but the Soviet Empire was one of them. It made the West suspicious that the USSR was intending to expand its borders. The first part of Churchill's 'Iron Curtain' speech, quoted earlier, shows this. Churchill himself did increase Stalin's distrust of the West by not opening the Second Front but he was not responsible for the brutality with which Stalin established the Soviet buffer zone, a brutality that, perhaps illogically, also increased the West's distrust of the USSR's territorial ambitions, especially as, like the USSR, its nerves were still jangling after the war against Nazism. I have argued in my co-authored book, *Britain and Soviet Communism*,[4] that the West's belief that the USSR was a military threat to Western Europe was ill-founded and influenced by Russophobic fears of Russian expansion that can be traced back to the nineteenth century. Nevertheless, although baseless, it was a real fear that influenced Western policymaking.

The USSR did not realise that its unwelcome presence in Eastern Europe was causing more trouble than it was worth. Far from being a strong defence (the East Europeans would have been unreliable), the Iron Curtain was in fact increasing the USSR's need for more armaments by alarming the West, which then poured billions of dollars into arming itself against a possible Communist attack. This forced the USSR into similar expenditure to arm itself against a hostile West and drained its coffers. The USA was better able to bear the financial burden than the USSR, having more resources and a smaller population.

The collapse of the Soviet Union

After Stalin's death in 1953, the USSR's control over Eastern Europe continued and its military spending increased. It has been estimated that by the mid-1980s the USSR was devoting between 15 per cent and 17 per cent of its GDP to this.[5] Obviously this was a huge drain on the USSR's resources. Moreover, it had to import grain to feed its growing population. Had it abandoned Stalin's policy of collectivised agriculture it might have returned to being an exporter of grain, as it was before the First World War. By 1985, because of its high military expenditure (which the invasion of Afghanistan increased), the fall in oil prices and the need to import grain, the USSR was near to financial collapse. This was the last scenario that Stalin and his successors had wanted for the Soviet Union.

The former Russian prime minister and distinguished economist Yegor Gaidar explained how the collapse of the Soviet Union occurred.[6] He said that in order buy grain abroad the USSR needed to export, but no one wanted its manufactured goods. Under Communism there had been no incentive to produce the quality consumer goods that capitalist societies wanted. Therefore the USSR had to export raw materials, in particular oil, to pay for the grain. Fortunately for the Soviet Union rich oil fields had been found in Western Siberia at the end of the 1960s, which it exploited, although it would have been better if it had been forced to reform and privatise its agriculture. Moreover, in the mid-1970s oil prices rose. The USSR could keep going so long as they remained high. But then in 1985 Saudi Arabia increased its oil production fourfold and the price of oil dropped. Gorbachev came to power in the USSR in that year and introduced his policies of 'perestroika' and 'glasnost', which opened up the economy and society. However, it was too late.

Due to the fall in the oil price, the USSR lost about $20 billion a year. Although it borrowed heavily, it was near to collapse. The Soviet Union received a warning from the Deutsche Bank that it would not be able to borrow more money from commercial banks. Instead it would have start negotiations with Western governments about so-called politically motivated credits: it would have to agree to political concessions in return for credit.[7]

Encouraged by Gorbachev's reforms, the East Europeans rose up to throw off the Soviet yoke. Gorbachev could not have stopped them even if he had wanted to, as then he would not have obtained credit from the West.

In December 1989 the USA's President George Bush met the USSR's President Gorbachev aboard a storm-lashed ship off Malta and effectively ended the Cold War. Gorbachev assured Bush he would never start a hot war, and Bush declared that they could transform the East-West relationship into one of lasting cooperation. A few weeks later the Communist governments in Eastern Europe were gone.

Although Gorbachev was seen as a hero in the West, the declining economic conditions in the USSR and slow pace of reforms led to his resignation and the breakup of the USSR in December 1991. The Soviet Union's expenditure on arms and grain and decreased oil revenues had emptied its coffers. Stalin had implemented the policy of forced collectivised agriculture, without which Russia could probably have exported grain as it had before the First World War. His establishing the Soviet bloc prompted the USA to produce arms with which the USSR had to compete. He thereby set the Soviet Union on the path to destruction, which was the last thing he had wanted.

Stalin's policies contained fatal flaws and were extreme, unethical and brutal. In China, Mao's policies were dramatically reversed after his death by the presence of liberals in the leadership. But this did not happen in Russia with Stalin's successors. They understandably did not want to give up the Soviet Empire as it was seen as essential to the USSR's defence. They could have changed the collectivised system of agriculture but they did not.

Therefore, the USSR had to import so much grain that it drained its wealth, as did its expenditure on armaments. More able leaders might have changed Stalin's policies, but Gorbachev did not appear on the scene until it was too late. Stalin must take the blame for his legacy, which did not make the USSR's collapse inevitable but highly probable.

Notes

1 Akhmatova, Anna, 'Requiem', http://www.poemhunter.com/poem/requiem.
2 Speech by Yegor Gaidar, www.aei.org/issue/foreign-and-defense-policy/regional/europe/the-soviet-collapse.
3 www.historyguide.org/europe/churchill.html.
4 Northedge, F. S. and Wells, Audrey, *Britain and Soviet Communism* (London 1982). The book argues against the idea of the 'Russian Threat'.
5 http://www.globalsecurity.org/military/world/russia/mo-budget.htm.
6 Gaidar, op. cit.
7 Ibid.

Further reading

Applebaum, Anne, *Iron Curtain: The Crushing of Eastern Europe 1944–56* (London 2012).
McAuley, Martin, *The Rise and Fall of the Soviet Union 1917–1991* (London 2007).

Section 4

The Second World War

8   France helped cause the Second World War

The last thing France wanted to do after the First World War was to provoke yet another one with Germany, but this is what it did by its treatment of that country at the peace conference afterwards. There has been much controversy over the effects of the Treaty of Versailles. It certainly did not make the Second World War inevitable as in the intervening years much happened and choices were freely made that could have avoided such an outcome. However, Hitler's vow to repudiate the hated Versailles Treaty and restore honour to Germany played an important part in his rise to power. The treaty also aroused the desire of many Germans to take revenge on France because it had dealt so harshly with Germany. The Versailles Treaty did not make the Second World War unavoidable but increased the probability of its outbreak.

At the Paris Peace Conference in 1919 France was determined not only to punish Germany for, as the French saw it, causing the First World War but also to avenge Germany's defeating France in 1871 in the Franco-Prussian War. Germany would therefore be so weakened that she would never again be a threat to France. Britain also wanted to punish Germany but the USA, represented by President Wilson, wanted a more constructive way to avoid war – namely, the establishment of the League of Nations. France was represented by its premier, Clemenceau, and Britain by its prime minister, Lloyd George. Clemenceau, under pressure from the French for revenge on Germany, presided over the conference as it was held in Paris.

The outcome of the conference's deliberations was the Treaty of Versailles, signed by the Allies and Germany in 1919. Germany was held 'solely' responsible for the war (blame which was difficult to justify historically) and therefore made to pay reparations for its cost. A commission, independent of the Allies' representatives, decided that Germany should pay £6,600 million compensation. Germany's armed forces were severely limited and no German troops were permitted in the Rhineland. Alsace-Lorraine was given to France. Germany lost further territory to Belgium, Denmark and Poland and was forbidden to unite with Austria. It also forfeited all its colonies.

On 13 July 1919, the Parisian newspaper *Le Petit Journal* published, on the front page of its illustrated supplement, a picture that showed how the French saw the peace treaty as their revenge. At the top of the page the vanquished French were depicted signing the peace treaty with Germany in 1871. Below it was a second picture of a humbled Germany signing the Treaty of Versailles in 1919 while a shining victorious France looks on. The picture was captioned 'A Ton Tour Germania!' (Your turn Germany!).[1]

At the peace conference Clemenceau argued, in addition to the other demands on Germany, that France should be given the Saar coalfields as Germany had deliberately damaged France's own. Wilson resisted this but Lloyd George came up with a compromise. The outcome was that, under a League of Nations mandate, France should occupy the Saar for fifteen years and then there should be a plebiscite as to its future. France would be paid compensation during the fifteen years by the Saar administration for the damage done to its own coal mines.

In 1923 the German government was unable to pay the reparations required under the Versailles Treaty. France and Belgium sent in troops to occupy the Ruhr, the centre of Germany's coal, iron and steel production. This further outraged the German people, who were undergoing an economic crisis and runaway inflation. The German government printed more money for the compensation but this led to hyperinflation. In November 1923 Adolf Hitler with members of the German Workers' Party attempted a 'putsch' in Munich against the German government, being enraged that it accepted the blame for the First World War and was bringing economic ruin on Germany. Hitler was arrested and charged with treason, his trial giving publicity to him and his cause. He served only nine months of his five-year sentence, during which time he wrote *Mein Kampf*. His life may well have been different had the crisis of 1923 not taken place. The next year the Dawes Plan made possible a more moderate system of repayment and the French and Belgian troops withdrew.

One writer who went to Germany in 1924 and witnessed the hatred of the Germans for France was Vera Brittain. In her *Testament of Youth* she records that the five commissioners appointed by the League of Nations to administer the Saar were regarded by the inhabitants 'as their oppressors': 'Local prophets had intimated to them on their arrival that within a month they would find a watery grave in the dirty depths of the Saar.'[2] She met a young German officer on a train who had expressed his desire to take revenge on the French: 'One day,' he exclaimed exultantly, 'we will make war upon them and treat them as they have treated us! I am longing for that war.'[3]

The Treaty of Versailles was a major factor in the rise of Hitler, who came to power vowing to repudiate the treaty, end the payment of reparations and restore honour to Germany. There were other causes in Hitler's rise, probably the most important being the colossal increase in unemployment, but the Treaty of Versailles was an important factor. The economic crisis alone could well have helped some socialist or communist parties to power, but national socialism appealed also to Germans angered over the peace treaty as well as unemployment.

However, there is some controversy as to the Treaty of Versailles's connection with the Second World War. The historian Margaret MacMillan remarked, 'Hitler did not wage war because of the Treaty of Versailles, although he found it a godsend for his propaganda.'[4] She argues that to regard the harsh terms of the peace treaty as ensuring a second world war 'is to ignore the actions of everyone – political leaders, diplomats, soldiers, ordinary voters – for twenty years between 1919 and 1939'.[5]

It is true that the Versailles Treaty did not make the Second World War inevitable, that much could have happened that could have avoided it. Nevertheless, the harshness of the treaty helped greatly to get Hitler into power in the first place, thus increasing the likelihood of a second war, although it did not make it unavoidable. Moreover, a desire for revenge can linger for decades, especially if the injustices remain. Hitler demonstrated this when the French surrendered in 1940.

MacMillan further claims that even if Germany had been left with the old borders, Hitler would still have wanted more. This argument is, of course, impossible to validate. Indeed, as has been pointed out earlier, Hitler might never have come to power had the Versailles Treaty left the old borders in place. Moreover it may have been the ease with which he regained the territories taken from Germany by the Versailles Treaty that encouraged him to try to gain even more. Britain in particular had thought that Germany had been dealt with unfairly in 1919 and at first did not oppose Hitler's recovery of former German territory. Moreover, many Germans no doubt wanted to avenge the suffering and shame of the German people caused by the peace treaty. The fact that they had been so badly treated might have spurred the Nazis to decide to greatly expand Germany's territory and make it larger and more powerful than it was before.

It has also been argued that the colossal compensation that Germany had to pay and the fact that it had to do this in cash rather than in goods, due to France's insistence, made Germany reliant on American loans, which partly paid for the reparations. When Wall Street crashed in 1929, so did Germany's economy, resulting in the high unemployment and runaway inflation that helped Hitler's rise to power. The economist John Maynard Keynes had warned, in *The Economic Consequences of the Peace* (1920), that the Versailles Treaty would not allow Germany's economy to recover and would cause European economic and political instability.[6] However, this argument is now regarded as highly debatable, although it has not been definitively refuted.

In 1939 Hitler invaded Poland, which both Britain and France had pledged to defend. They therefore declared war on Germany. In 1940 Germany invaded France, which surrendered and had to sign the armistice in a place deliberately chosen by Hitler to mark Germany's revenge: the Compiegne Forest, the site of the 1918 armistice, in the very same railway carriage used for the signing of the armistice. The carriage was removed from a museum and placed in the same spot where it had been during the 1918 armistice signing. Hitler then sat in the same chair in the carriage where Marshal Foch had sat at the beginning of armistice negotiations in 1918. After listening to the reading of the preamble of the armistice he then left the carriage just as Foch had done in 1918, showing disdain for the Germans. So Hitler showed the same for the French. The Germans' revenge was complete. This was the last thing had France wanted, of course, but it had partly brought it on itself by its own vengeful policy towards Germany.

Notes

1 www.gallica.bnf.fr/, *Le Petit Journal*, Supplement du Dimanche, 13-07-1919.
2 Brittain, Vera, *Testament of Youth* (London 1933), p. 630.
3 Ibid., p. 640.
4 MacMillan, Margaret, *Paris 1919* (New York 2002), p. 493.
5 Ibid.
6 Hobsbawm, Eric, *The Age of Extremes* (London 1994), p. 99.

9   Churchill helped cause the Blitz

The last thing that Britain wanted in the Second World War was for its civilian areas to be heavily bombed by the Germans, but this is what happened as revenge for Churchill's retaliation for a German mistake. On the night of 24 August 1940 the Luftwaffe, aiming for RAF airfields and oil depots, accidentally dropped some bombs over London, killing civilians. This was against Hitler's orders.[1] Hitler and Goring then issued commands to the Luftwaffe forbidding the bombing of London.[2] Probably not realising this, Churchill ordered the retaliatory bombing of Berlin. Military and industrial sites were targeted, but some civilian areas were also hit by mistake, due to poor visibility. Hitler replied with the Blitz, which might not have happened had Churchill not sunk to the level of mere retaliation. Thousands of lives were then unnecessarily lost during the war as each side bombed the other's cities.

Notes

1 www.bbc.co.uk/history/worldwars/wwtwo/area bombing; Bishop, Patrick, *Battle of Britain* (London 2009), p. 213.
2 www.battleofbritain1940.net.

Section 5

Genocide

10 Hitler and the Nazis created Israel

The last thing that Hitler and the Nazis wanted to achieve was the creation of the state of Israel, but this is what they ironically played a crucial role in bringing about through their evil persecution of the Jews.

To Hitler, the creation of a Jewish state was anathema. In *Mein Kampf* (published in 1925) he wrote that the Jews did not want a state:

> for the purpose of living there; all they want is a central organisation for their international world swindle, endowed with its own sovereign rights and removed from the intervention of other states; a haven for convicted scoundrels and a university for budding crooks.[1]

Other Nazi leaders echoed this view after they came to power. In 1937, the Nazi foreign minister Von Neurath declared that a Jewish state would not be in Germany's interests. It would provide an 'internationally recognised power base for international Jewry rather like the Vatican state for political Catholicism or Moscow for the Comintern'.[2] However, it was the Nazis' extreme anti-Semitic persecution that drove Jews unwillingly from Europe into Palestine in such large numbers that the state of Israel became possible. Furthermore, the Nazis forced people of Jewish extraction who did not think of themselves as Jews to regard themselves as such and not as Europeans, thereby helping the Zionists' cause. Moreover the Nazis' Haavara agreement with the Zionists, encouraging Jews to go to Palestine in the 1930s with part of their capital, helped to lay the foundations of the Israeli economy, as well as to increase the number of Jews in Palestine who would have preferred to go to another country if given the chance. Finally the Holocaust aroused global sympathy for the Jews and for the idea of the Jewish state as their place of refuge.

Zionism by itself did not create Israel in 1948. The Nazis' crucifixion of the Jews was essential to Israel's resurrection. We must therefore first look at the Zionists' attempt to build a Jewish state in Palestine before the Nazis came to power in 1933.

Zionism

Zionism, derived from the biblical term for Jerusalem, was a Jewish nationalist movement that developed in the nineteenth century alongside other European nationalist movements. It encouraged Jews to emigrate to Palestine, where they hoped to establish their own state, free from persecution, in the 'Promised Land'. However, the Zionists had a problem: most Jews, especially in Western Europe, did not want to go there.

With the Enlightenment and the Industrial Revolution Jews had been assimilated into Western European society and could enter the professions and politics. Having for centuries earlier been forced into moneylending and trade, many Jews now prospered as owners of banking-houses and businesses.

On the other hand Palestine, part of the Ottoman Empire, was an inhospitable, underdeveloped land. While at every Passover Seder Jews would say, 'Next year in Jerusalem', the reality was that if they emigrated anywhere, it would be to the land of opportunity: the USA. Many did not want even that as, now emancipated, they preferred the comforts and culture of European life. Some did not even think of themselves as Jews.

However, in Eastern Europe the situation was different. Thousands of Jews were still being killed in horrific pogroms there. Many of them fled to Palestine from the 1880s onwards and there, inspired by socialist ideals, set up 'kibbutzim', where Jews worked for the good of the agricultural collective. Among them was one David Grun, who became the leader of the 'yishuv', the Palestinian Jewish community and later, having changed his name to Ben-Gurion, was to become Israel's first prime minister.

Nevertheless, by 1917 the yishuv (or Jewish community) in Palestine still made up only 8 per cent of the population which consisted mainly of Arabs.[3] In that year the Jews did obtain the Balfour Declaration but that did not result in greatly increased Jewish emigration to Palestine. Issued by the British foreign secretary, Lord Balfour, in response to Jewish lobbying, the declaration stated that 'His Majesty's Government views with favour the establishment in Palestine of a national home for the Jewish people.'[4] Britain had not at this time declared its support for 'a Jewish state' but only 'a national home' and not even 'the' national home for the Jews. The declaration had added that nothing shall be done which 'may prejudice the civil and religious right of existing non-Jewish communities in Palestine'.

After the First World War Britain was given a mandate over Palestine by the League of Nations and in 1920 a British civilian administration was set up. But the Jews themselves did not flock to Palestine. In 1922 the Jewish population in Palestine made up only 11 per cent of the total, 83,000 out of 725,000.[5] During the years 1923 to 1929 Jewish immigration actually dropped. In 1927 there was no Jewish immigration and in 1928 it was net only ten persons.[6]

The existence of the Balfour Declaration and the British civilian administration in Palestine did encourage Jews to flee there after the Nazis came to power, but not before.

Nazi anti-Semitic persecution

Anti-Semitism had run deep in Europe ever since the Jews had arrived there after fleeing from Roman persecution in the first and second centuries AD. The Christian Church had illogically perceived all Jews for all time as 'Christ-killers'. Resentment of the Jews was also later fuelled by the envy of their success in trade and banking, which had resulted from their earlier being restricted to earning their money from moneylending and commerce. Moreover after the First World War many Germans blamed the Jews for Germany's military defeat.

The Nazis were attracted by the racial theories of Gobineau, a nineteenth-century French writer who argued that people can be divided into races of unequal ability. Influenced by Nietzsche's idea of the superman, the Nazis developed the theory that there existed a blond, blue-eyed Aryan master race to which they belonged, despite the fact that some Nazi leaders did not fit this stereotype, including Hitler himself.

The Jews, by contrast, were branded by the Nazis as 'subhuman', yet also as the trouble-making driving forces behind not only communism but also its antithesis, capitalism. The Nazis, of course, totally denied the great intellectual contributions of Jews to the world and claimed they were undermining German culture.

Moreover there was a strong Nazi belief that there was a conspiracy by the Jews to dominate the world. The Nazis were greatly influenced by the 'Protocols of the Elders of Zion', which was a document purporting to describe a plan by the Jews to achieve global domination. It was first published in 1903 in the Russian Empire and widely circulated in the West, where it was revealed to be a complete forgery by the *Times* in London in 1921. Hitler nevertheless endorsed it as authentic in his book *Mein Kampf*, which was published in 1925.

The actual and official discrimination against the Jews by the Nazis began as soon as they came to power in Germany in January 1933.Therefore Jews worldwide launched in March of that year an international boycott against German goods and against loans to Germany. In London, on

24 March 1933, the *Daily Express* summed up the news with a banner head-line: 'Judea Declares War on Germany'. The boycott by the Jews outside Germany lasted until 1939. Whether it encouraged or undermined the subse-quent anti-Semitic policies of the Nazis, already deeply prejudiced, cannot be determined.

The Nazis retaliated with a one-day boycott of Jewish businesses and professionals on 1 April 1933. The SA or the storm troopers, the Nazi private army, stood outside Jewish stores with posters declaring, 'Germans, defend yourselves! Do not buy from Jews.' Yellow and black stars of David were painted on Jewish shopfronts, which were sometimes broken.

On 7 April 1933 employment in the German civil service was restricted to 'Aryans'. Jews were expelled from it, so that they could not be teachers, judges or university lecturers. On the same day Jewish lawyers were denied the right to be admitted to the Bar and the right to practise law if they were already members. Jewish books were burned along with those of others whom the Nazis disliked.

On 15 September 1935 the Nuremberg Laws were passed, removing citi-zenship rights from Jews and forbidding their marriage to Germans. In addi-tion all Jews had to wear the yellow Star of David on their coats to show they were non-Germans. All of this persecution inadvertently helped the Zionist cause by forcing Jews to regard themselves as non-Europeans and feel uncomfortable in Germany. Furthermore, as they could not marry non-Jews, the sense of a Jewish race was strengthened.

On 14 November 1935 the Nazis issued their definition of a Jew. This was anyone with three Jewish grandparents or someone with two Jewish grand-parents who belonged to the Jewish community on 15 September 1935 or who joined afterwards. Persons of mixed blood were called 'hybrids' of the first degree if they had two Jewish grandparents or 'hybrids' of the second degree if one grandparent was Jewish.

To locate the people they believed were members of the Jewish race, there being no blood test, the Nazis had to rely on genealogical documentation and evidence of marriages in synagogues. Their investigations were very efficient in tracing their victims, using IBM's punch card technology to col-late their findings.

In *Mein Kampf*, Hitler argued that Jews were identified by a common blood, not by a religious faith: 'The Jew has always been a people with definite racial characteristics and not a religion.'[7] Showing great ignorance of the Jewish faith, he claimed that the religious aspect consisted mainly of practices to keep the Jewish blood pure.

This belief that Jews were a race rather than a religion became an important plank in Nazi anti-Semitism. Yet Nazi racial persecution ironically helped the Zionist cause by making secular and religious Jews think of themselves as one non-European people who could not be assimilated into Germany. The Nazis forced a Jewish consciousness on those of Jewish extraction but not of the Jewish faith who had previously thought of themselves as German. This was an important contribution to the building up of the people who were later to form the state of Israel. (In fact whether Jews do actually share a common blood is still a debatable matter.)

As the Nazis tried to drive out of Germany all those they regarded as Jewish, Goebbels' Ministry of Propaganda poured out anti-Semitic poison, blaming the Jews for Germany's problems. Public notices were put up informing Jews they were not welcome. Jewish children had to be educated in Jewish schools and the number of Jewish university students was limited. Nevertheless, until the Second World War the Nazis' plan was not to exterminate the Jews, but to force them to leave Germany so that it was 'Judenrein' ('Jew-free').

The Transfer Agreement or 'Haavara'

The Nazis not only drove the Jews from Germany by persecution but also actually encouraged them to emigrate to Palestine through the 'Haavara' or 'Transfer Agreement', which was made surprisingly between the Zionists and the Nazis.

The agreement meant that German Jews, emigrating to Palestine, would be able to buy from Germany, with part of their capital that was otherwise blocked there, machinery for farming, building houses, roads and so on; luxury goods, such as perfumes, artificial silks and women's stockings, could also be bought.[8] In this way the Nazis inadvertently helped to build up the economy of the Palestinian Jewish community. The Jews could not use their capital in Germany in this way if they went to countries other than Palestine. Further, the immigrant's fee of one thousand Palestine pounds that the British government required could more easily be paid.

The Haavara was actually being negotiated before the Nazis came to power by Palestinian Jews and the German government. The Nazis agreed to the Transfer Agreement because they wanted the Jews to leave Germany, which, through the Haavara, would not lose the Jews' capital as the portion they could use had to be spent on German goods. Moreover, it meant that the international Jewish boycott of German goods, begun in March 1933, was now broken.[9]

For their part, the Zionists wanted the Transfer Agreement because it meant more German Jews emigrating to Palestine, where their funds would strengthen the economy of the Palestinian Jewish community.

In 1939 the Transfer Agreement ended with the outbreak of war. By this time it had contributed to the Palestinian Jewish community both in terms of enlarging its population and of strengthening its economy.

I shall now look at the increase in Jewish emigration to Palestine during this period.

Palestine in the 1930s

In the early 1930s Jews were attracted to the growing citrus industry in Palestine at a time when work was scarce in the Depression-hit West. Between 1930 and 1933, the number of legal Jewish immigrants (from Germany and other countries) into Palestine rose from 4,000 in 1930 to 30,000 in 1933.[10] In that year the number of German Jews legally entering Palestine was 7,600. As Nazi persecution increased and as the Transfer Agreement facilitated the Jews' moving to Palestine, so Jewish immigration increased. In 1934 this rose to 9,800, which was about a quarter of the total number of Jewish immigrants into that country in that year. In 1935 61,000 Jews immigrated into Palestine, the actual number of German Jews being 8,600. The next year 8,700 German Jews went to Palestine, the total number of Jewish immigrants being 29,700.[11] More Jews entered Palestine illegally.

It was not only the Nazis who drove the Jews to Palestine at this time. More Jews flooded into Palestine from Poland (where there was a large Jewish population) to escape anti-Semitism there.[12] But later the shadow of Nazism spreading over Europe caused thousands of Jews to flee to the 'Promised Land'.

By 1936 the Palestinian Arabs were alarmed, fearing that they would be swamped by floods of Jews that the British would do nothing to stop. Moreover the Arabs were aware of Zionist arms smuggling. Therefore between 1936 and 1938 the Arabs rose in revolt against the British Mandate.

In response, the British sent out, in 1937, a commission of enquiry headed by Lord Peel. This recommended partitioning Palestine into two states, one for the Jews and one for the Arabs. Jewish immigration was to be limited to 12,000 for the next five years and Jerusalem and Haifa were to remain under the British Mandate. The Zionists were disappointed at the limitation to Jewish immigration but delighted at the fact the British government had for the first time actually spoken of a 'Jewish state'. This it would not have done if the Palestinian Jewish population had not expanded considerably in the 1930s. The Palestinian Arabs, for their part, were incensed but Britain crushed their revolt. However, in 1938 a League of Nations technical commission declared the partition plan unworkable.

Events in Europe in 1938 increased Jewish emigration. In March the Nazis took over Austria and made the Jews immediately unwelcome through the harsh policies of Adolf Eichmann's Central Office for Jewish Emigration set up in Vienna, and later in Berlin.

Kristallnacht (Night of Broken Glass)

In November 1938 the anti-Semitic violence of Kristallnacht occurred, following the assassination of a German diplomat in Paris by a Jew. Nazi militants attacked Jewish shops, offices, homes and synagogues. Nearly 100 Jews were killed and 30,000 were sent to concentration camps. The Jewish community was fined one billion marks, forbidden to run businesses or to employ Germans. Jewish children were expelled from schools. Britain agreed to take 10,000 Jewish children under the Kindertransport plan.

Many German Jews until this time still hoped the anti-Semitic persecution would pass. Kristallnacht made them change their minds. As one former Jewish refugee with the Kindertransport recollected,

> Everyone understood that they ought to be emigrating, but it was only when the watershed of Kristallnacht occurred in November 1938 that my parents, in common with ninety per cent of other German Jews, thought: it's no good staying, they're going to kill us.[13]

Palestine now seemed a more desirable refuge to German Jews. In 1939 the number of Jews emigrating from Germany to Palestine rose to nearly 8,500, double the totals for 1937 and 1938.[14]

The Second World War and the Holocaust

If Kristallnacht was the stimulus to German Jewish emigration, the Second World War and the Holocaust provided the final push to the Jewish state. It was the Nazi jackboot that kicked the 'Chosen People' back into the 'Promised Land'.

In January 1939 Hitler told the Reichstag that Europe would never be at peace until the Jewish question was solved. He believed that this could be achieved if the Jews turned to 'respectable, constructive work', but that

> If the international finance-Jewry in and outside Europe should succeed in plunging the nations once more into a world war, then the result will be not the Bolshevisation of the earth, and thus the victory of Jewry, but the annihilation of the Jewish race in Europe.[15]

It was, however, Hitler himself who plunged the nations into war. In March 1939 he occupied the rest of Czechoslovakia, having obtained the Sudetenland in the Munich Conference in 1938. In September 1939 he attacked Poland. Therefore Britain and France, which had guaranteed the integrity of Poland's borders, declared war on Germany. During the invasion of Poland the Nazis used 'Einsatzgruppen' to terrorise and murder Jews, who were forced into ghettoes. These mobile killing units were also used when Hitler invaded the USSR in June 1941 and were sent to massacre Jews in German-occupied areas. Meanwhile, as the Nazis extended their occupation of Europe, so their concentration camp system also expanded. These camps had been set up in the 1930s to deal with those whom the Nazis perceived as their opponents, such as Jews and communists, but they were not extermination camps. During the Second World War more camps were built in Eastern Europe; some were slave-labour camps for minorities, such as gypsies as well as Jews, but others, in Poland, such as Sobibor and Treblinka, were extermination camps only for Jews. Auschwitz was a combined slave-labour and extermination camp mainly, but not solely, for Jews, of whom almost a million died at the camp.

At the Wannsee Conference on 20 January 1942, senior Nazi officials (but not the Nazi leaders) discussed the practical measures involved in the 'Final Solution': the total annihilation of the European Jews.

The Final Solution resulted in an attempt at genocide on an industrial scale never before witnessed. It meant the massacre of millions of innocent Jewish men, women and children. By the end of the Second World War two out of every three European Jews, approximately six million of them, had been killed by the Nazis, whose systematic method of mass murder demonstrated that it was they themselves who were 'subhuman', not their victims. Indeed, it was a back-handed compliment to the abilities of the Jews that so much of the Nazis' time and energies were spent on trying to exterminate them as a perceived threat.

Britain and the USA were alerted by reports from Eastern Europe as to the Jews' fate but, partly because the Depression had caused high unemployment, they refused to allow more of them into their countries as refugees. Appalled by this, the Anglican Church leadership attempted to intervene. On 23 March 1943 in the House of Lords the archbishop of Canterbury, William Temple, proposed that 'through a neutral power, an offer be made to the Nazi government whereby Britain would receive so many Jews each month into the lands of the British Empire and that of its allies'.[16] But this suggestion was not acted upon by the British government, nor were those of others. At the time of the Jews' greatest need the West's response to their plight was inadequate. This turned the Jews worldwide to support Zionism, realising the need for a Jewish state as a place of refuge from the cruelty of the world that had abandoned them.

Palestine after 1939

As war approached in 1939 Britain was concerned to keep the support of the Arabs and their oil. In a white paper it therefore limited Jewish immigration into Palestine to 15,000 a year for the next five years. In response, Zionists in Palestine attacked the British presence there. In New York, in 1942, David Ben-Gurion and the Zionists adopted a programme at the Biltmore Hotel providing for unrestricted Jewish immigration to Palestine, which was to become a Jewish commonwealth.

After the war, the full revelation of the Nazis' attempt to exterminate the Jewish people resulted in worldwide sympathy for the Zionists' goal of a Jewish state. The sympathy would not have existed had not the Jews suffered at the hands of the Nazis. Support for a Jewish state was particularly important in the USA (where Jews had not initially been interested in Zionism) since it was able to pressure Britain. The cost of the war had made Britain financially dependent on the USA, which was demanding that Britain allow massive Jewish immigration into Palestine.

Despite British attempts to limit Jewish immigration to Palestine, the Jews during the war and afterwards found their way by often desperate methods into that country. By 1947 they made up approximately one third of the Palestinian population,[17] compared to being only one tenth in the 1920s. With this size their claims to statehood seemed more realistic.

In February 1947, with hostilities between Jews and Arabs continuing, Britain bowed to the USA's pressure and handed the Palestine problem over to the UN. The UN created a Special Commission on Palestine, which proposed partition into Jewish and Arab states. On 29 November the UN voted on the proposal, Resolution 181, which was passed.

However, the Arabs did not accept that the UN had the authority to partition the country. Further, they believed that it was manifestly unfair to give the Jews 56 per cent of the land (owing to the distribution of settlements) since they made up only one third of the population of Palestine.

The date set for partition was 14 May 1948. On that day the Declaration of Independence of the State of Israel was proclaimed by David Ben-Gurion, who was to become the first prime minister of the country.

A Jewish state had been made possible because Nazi persecution had driven to Palestine great numbers of Jews who would not otherwise have left Europe. They had enlarged the Jewish community in Palestine so that it could seriously claim statehood.

Furthermore, Nazi persecution, especially the Holocaust, had aroused global support for a Jewish state, importantly in the USA. Had the Jews not suffered in extremity, the state of Israel would not have been established when it was, if ever at all.

The Transfer Agreement had encouraged Jews to go to Palestine with their funds, which built up the population and the economy of the future Jewish state, but without the Nazis' drive to make Germany 'Judenrein', most German Jews would not have regarded emigration to Palestine as an attractive idea.

The Zionists' drive, organisation and leadership were remarkable, but without the huge increase in Jewish emigration to Palestine from the Nazi threat, the state of Israel would not have been established when it was. Moreover the Nazis achieved what the Zionists wanted to do but could not: the forcing of Europeans of Jewish extraction who did not regard themselves as Jews to regard themselves as such and to join the ranks of the Jews fleeing to Palestine.

Ironically the Nazis gathered up the fragments of the Jewish people scattered in Europe and poured them into Palestine, where they formed the living mosaic of Israel.

By their heinous acts the Nazis created the opposite of what they had intended. The ancient state of Israel was resurrected after the crucifixion of the Jews. Evil was providentially turned into potential good.

Notes

1   http://www.hitler.org/writings/meinkampf/mkvich11.html, p. 27.
2   Nicosia, Francis R., *The Third Reich and the Palestine Question* (London 1985), p. 121.
3   Goldberg, David J., *To the Promised Land: A History of Zionist Thought* (London 1996), p. 148.
4   http://www.jewishvirtuallibrary.org/isource/history/balfour.html.
5   Shanin, Teodar, 'The Zionisms of Israel', in *Ideology in the Middle East and Pakistan*, ed. By Fred Halliday and Hamza Alavi (London 1988), p. 226.
6   Mansfield, Peter, *A History of the Middle East* (Harmondsworth, England 1992), p. 204.
7   http://www.hitler.org/writings/meinkampf/mkulch11.html.
8   Nicosia, op. cit., pp. 208–9 (all reference to the Transfer Agreement is drawn from this work).
9   Ibid., p. 54.
10 Mansfield, op. cit., p. 205.
11 Nicosia, op. cit., Appendix 7.
12 'British Mandate: A Survey of Palestine', prepared by the British Mandate for the UN, Vol. 1, p. 187, http://www.palestineremembered.com/articles/a-survey-of-palestine/story6628.html.
13 Smith, Lyn, *Forgotten Voices of the Holocaust* (London 2005), p. 57.
14 Nicosia, op. cit., Appendix 7.
15 http://www.holocaust-history.org/der-ewige-jude/hitler-19390130.shtml.
16 Hansard, 23 March 1943, http://hansard.millbanksystems.com/lords/1943/mar/23/german-atrocities-aid-for-refugees.
17 Mansfield, Peter, *The Arabs* (Harmondsworth, England 1988), p. 237.

11 Genocide backfired in Bosnia and Kosovo

Genocide was defined in 1948 by the UN General Assembly's 'Convention on the Prevention and Punishment of the Crime of Genocide' as acts committed 'with intent to destroy, in whole or in part, a national, ethnical or racial or religious group'. Genocide usually fails to accomplish its goals, but rarely so dramatically as in the Nazis' attempt to exterminate the Jews, which produced results completely opposite to those intended: the emergence of the state of Israel. This was a partly due to the fact that the Zionists were able courageously to organise an exodus of their people to a land that they believed was theirs and was well outside the enemy's control. However, for other ethnic groups similarly persecuted this was not possible.

Bosnia

In Bosnia the last thing the Serb leaders wanted was to end up as prisoners accused of war crimes and genocide at the International Criminal Court while their dream of a 'Greater Serbia' had vanished and Muslims and Croats thrived in the independent state of Bosnia. But this is what happened as the Serbs' actions against the Bosnian Muslims were so heinous that NATO was prompted to intervene.

In 1992, during the civil war following the breakup of Yugoslavia, the Bosnian Serbs, backed by Serbia, tried to ethnically cleanse Bosnia of its Muslims and Croats. Srebrenica was declared a UN safe area but the Serbs massacred 7,500 Muslim men they took from there. They subsequently shelled the crowded marketplace in Sarajevo, killing forty civilians. This was the final straw for NATO (which was not fully aware of the extent of the massacre). It carried out airstrikes against the Serb troops, which eventually led to peace negotiations, the arrest of Serb leaders, who were charged with war crimes and genocide, and the division of Bosnia into a Croat-Muslim Federation (for Bosnian Croats and Muslims) and the Republik Srpska (for Bosnia Serbs).

The Serbs' evil actions were so extreme that they backfired, prompting NATO to intervene on behalf of the Muslims. This Western intervention was ethical and did not backfire. Nevertheless, Muslims in particular have criticised the West for not intervening earlier in Bosnia, where some of them have become radicalised.

Kosovo

The West also successfully intervened to stop Serbia from massacring the Muslim Kosovars. Without UN approval, in 1999 NATO intervened with a bombing campaign that forced the Serbs to stop trying to ethnically cleanse the Albanians from Kosovo. Whether it was illegal but morally justified is still controversial. The British prime minister Tony Blair justified NATO's action in a speech that he made at Chicago University when he invoked the principle of the Responsibility to Protect. This was later known as R2P and was endorsed by the UN General Assembly in 2005.

At the war's end, about 10,000 civilians had been killed and hundreds of thousands had become refugees. Serb military leaders were charged at The Hague with crimes against humanity during the conflict in Kosovo.

However, for other ethnic groups elsewhere in the world foreign protection was not forthcoming.

Further reading

Glenny, Misha, *The Balkans Nationalism, War and the Great Powers 1804–1999* (London 1999).
Glenny, Misha, *The Fall of Yugoslavia* (London 1996).

Section 6

Massacres with apparently no reverse results

12 Rwanda, Cambodia, Sri Lanka, Darfur and ISIS

Not all evil policies seem to produce reverse results, as the aftermaths of governmental massacres in Rwanda, Cambodia, Sri Lanka and Darfur have shown. In the last three examples there may be a backlash later. The massacres may not have yet backfired on the perpetrators because the latter can subjugate the people with brutal power at the moment.

In Rwanda 500,000 people, mainly Tutsis, were killed by Hutus in 1994. Although the Hutus' motives were evil, and although they were finally defeated by the Tutsis' 'Rwanda Patriotic Front', the outcome was not the complete opposite of the Hutu's intentions. Indeed it could be said that the situation is better than that as the Tutsis and Hutus seem now to work together. This may be due to the fact that a government of national unity was formed after the conflict, but most importantly because of the use of the community-based 'gacaca' court system, where respected elders endeavoured to effect some kind of truth and justice, resulting in no obvious backlash.

In Cambodia the Khmer Rouge killed nearly 2 million people in Cambodia during the mid-1970s but there were no obvious reverse results (although some of the leaders were brought to an international tribunal and charged with genocide) probably because the succeeding government forced the perpetrators of genocide and their victims' families to live together in a form of national amnesia.

In Sri Lanka, the UN estimates that 40,000 civilians, as well as thousands of Tamil and Sinhalese soldiers, lost their lives in Sri Lanka during the final phase of the civil war in 2009.[1] Both sides had committed atrocities but the Sri Lankan government in particular had clearly committed war crimes, for which it has not been brought to account. Its unethical actions may prove counterproductive in the long term, but immediately are not apparent because of government control.

In Darfur in Sudan the government is supporting Arab militias, known as 'Janjaweed', to crush the African farmers' rebel movements in a struggle for resources. The resulting massacres do not seem to have backfired on the government.

Thus, mass murders are still being carried out by governments, seemingly with immunity. Whether this will remain so is yet to be discovered.

ISIS

A brief mention should be made here of ISIS, or so-called Islamic State of Iraq, which is not a state nor does it have a government, but its seeming ability to massacre civilians without retribution demands comment. (Its rise has been described in Chapter 2.) This Sunni Islamic extremist group is aiming to establish a worldwide caliphate through bloodshed and terror. In 2016 it seems still unchecked, but its violent methods are probably going to prove counterproductive.

Note

1 www.deccanchronicle.com/loss-of life, Sri Lanka, 19 September 2014.

Section 7

Further unethical policies that have not produced reverse results

13 American imperialism in Latin America – exception Cuba

It seems that where an empire has the overwhelming power to oppress other states for decades, reverse results, the opposite of its goals of economic and political exploitation, do not seem to occur. This could be because, as in the case of Latin America, the oppressed states or left-wing movements were too weak to fight back. Had they been driven by the USA's interventions to turn fully to communism and then been strongly supported by the USSR, they might have been able to turn the tables on the USA, which did fear they already were thus influenced: but they were not. This is not to argue that communism in Latin America would have been good for it but it is an explanation of why the rule of reverse results did not apply there, other than in Cuba, although, there could, of course, be delayed results from the USA's intervention in Latin America.

In Guatemala and in Chile, the USA actually overthrew democratically elected governments, fearing its commercial and strategic interests were threatened, and caused immense suffering and loss of life. America has not seemed to suffer from the consequences.

Cuba

However, in Cuba the USA's policies did backfire. Castro was not a Marxist-Leninist when he came to power in 1959, overthrowing the corrupt Cuban dictator, Fulgencio Batista, who had allowed the country to become a rich man's playground. Castro helped the exploited landless poor by carrying out land reform, but this threatened the interests of American owners of sugar plantations there. Therefore the USA embarked on a series of punitive measures, such as embargos on sugar, oil and guns, but this merely drove Castro to buy them from the USSR.

After more counterproductive responses, in January 1961, the USA broke off diplomatic relations with Cuba. In the April 1961 the USA sponsored the

Bay of Pigs invasion by Cuban exiles. It was a disaster as the Cuban people, pleased with Castro's reforms, refused to rise up against him. When on 1 May Castro called the revolution in Cuba 'socialist', it was clear that the USA had driven the island on its doorstep into the arms of the USSR, which was the opposite of what it had intended.

14 Recent European imperialism

Recent European empires do not seem to have suffered from their colonisation policies backfiring on them either, despite the sometimes extreme exploitation and oppression involved.

It was Hitler, a despiser of the Asian and African native peoples, who unwittingly greatly helped them gain their independence by waging war on the European imperialists. The Second World War left the latter so severely weakened that they could not subjugate their colonies when these began fighting for independence.

The imperial attempts to crush the native uprisings ultimately failed, but this did not mean that the colonial policies boomeranged. Nevertheless, it is true that the latter's failure to develop their colonies' economies by encouraging manufacturing, leaving them instead dependent on exporting raw materials and crops at prices set by the former imperial powers, has had also adverse effects on the First World. The resulting poverty in developing countries has led to social unrest, conflicts, religious extremism, environmental degradation, drug trafficking and an inability buy exports from the wealthier countries. Further, the desperate floods of illegal migrants into Europe who are fleeing conflict and poverty are partly a product of Western imperial policies in their lands.

In certain countries where the rule of reverse results might have been expected to prevail in the form of revenge against imperialists, it did not, owing to the leadership of certain individuals. In India there could have been a more bloody conflict against Britain from the 1920s if the Indian nationalist movement had been led by a militant, vengeful man, unlike the non-violent Gandhi.

In Africa white settlers in many colonies faced violence and were eventually forced to leave. In South Africa a bloodbath of recrimination might have been expected, where Afrikaners experienced black revenge and the reverse of the goals of the apartheid system. However, this did not happen due to the leadership of Nelson Mandela and other members of the African National

Congress (ANC), who set up the Truth and Reconciliation Commission and led the people to peaceful democracy and forgiveness.

Mahatma Gandhi and Nelson Mandela, together with Robert Schuman, who led France and Germany to reconciliation in the EEC, will be considered in the next chapters.

Section 8

Peacemakers with positive results

15 Mahatma Gandhi and non-violent protest

In the next three chapters I shall consider three peacemakers whose ethical policies, while extreme, have had no unintended negative reverse results but, in fact, have changed the world for the better. Indeed, their moral leadership prevented the rule of reverse results from being played out in a harmful way. These leaders are Mahatma Gandhi, whose example of peaceful protest has influenced generations of resisters to oppression and thereby saved lives; Nelson Mandela, whose policy of reconciliation after the collapse of apartheid avoided much bloodshed; and Robert Schuman, who devoted his political life after the Second World War to preventing another such conflict ever breaking out again and thereby became the 'founding father' of the European Community. What has distinguished these men is that their motives for their policies were highly and clearly moral, unlike those of many politicians and governments who find that their actions eventually boomerang to their detriment. The non-violent policies of Gandhi, Mandela and Schuman have not backfired but shine as a guide to a higher level of human behaviour. The background to the development of their political ideas must therefore be considered.

Gandhi

Einstein once said of Gandhi, 'Generations to come, it may be, will scarcely believe that such a one as this ever in flesh and blood walked upon this earth.'[1] Gandhi's leadership of the Indian nationalist movement was highly ethical in that it was non-violent and well-justified opposition to British imperial rule in India. It certainly did not result in the reverse of what Gandhi had intended. It pressured the British to leave India but did not use violence against them, although they responded violently to Indian demonstrations. As a result, Gandhi shone as ethically superior to his imperial masters, winning worldwide respect. Consequently his method of peaceful resistance to oppression has been copied by protest movements throughout the world.

This is what Gandhi would have wanted as he believed his method was the right way to resolve all conflicts, even though it might mean death for some protestors.

While it was the Second World War's draining Britain's coffers that finally forced the British to leave India, Gandhi's movement did the groundwork for their departure and no doubt would have eventually obliged them to go. The need to arrest and jail thousands Indian protestors put a huge strain on Britain's resources as did the withdrawal of the Indians' labour and cooperation on which the Raj depended. In the words of the distinguished historian of India, Judith Brown, Gandhi's protests 'challenged the very nature of British imperialism, and were designed to undermine the implicit Indian cooperation on which imperial rule rested'.[2] Moreover Gandhi's non-violent resistance movement united the Indians across creed, class and caste. As Professor Brown points out, he built up 'the Congress into a mass-based party which was capable of mounting both a moral and a physical challenge to the Raj, and eventually forming the government of a new nation'.[3]

Early development of Gandhi's thought

Mohandas Gandhi was born in 1869 in Gujarat to a merchant Hindu family. His father was a government official and his mother a particularly devout Hindu. In 1888 he went to study law at the Inns of Court in London. In that city surprisingly his Hindu faith was developed as well as his understanding of Christianity. There he met members of the Theosophy Society, who inspired him to read the Bhagavad Gita, which he had not read back home in India.

Gandhi also joined the Vegetarian Society, which strengthened his Hindu beliefs on this issue. It was, in fact, at a vegetarian boarding house that he met a man who was to change his life. This nameless man was a Christian who encouraged him to read the Bible. Through him Gandhi first came across Jesus's 'Sermon on the Mount' with its exhortation to 'turn the other cheek' and not retaliate. This was the genesis of Gandhi's non-violent protest beliefs.[4]

'Satyagraha'

In 1891 Gandhi returned to India to practise his profession, but in 1893 he accepted a post with an Indian law firm in Durban, South Africa. There he was angered at the way Indians were treated, so he devoted much of his time to fighting discriminatory legislation. While he was doing so he developed his distinctive method of non-violent protest, which he called 'satyagraha' or 'truth force' or 'firmness in truth' ('satya' means 'truth' and 'agraha' is 'firmness of force'). It was this principle that Gandhi used later to resist the British presence in India itself.

In 1909 he wrote a pamphlet, 'Hind Swaraj' or 'Home Rule for India', arguing for passive resistance against the British. He explained that the object was not to make the British suffer as the Indians would suffer because 'Passive resistance is a method of securing rights by personal suffering, it is the reverse of resistance by arms.'[5] He asserted:

> Passive resistance is an all-sided sword, it can be used anyhow; it blesses him who uses it and him against whom it is used. Without drawing a drop of blood it produces far reaching results. It never rusts and cannot be stolen.[6]

Influence of Jesus Christ's teaching

In developing his non-violent form of protest, Gandhi was greatly influenced by the teachings of Jesus Christ, although he would never describe himself as a Christian, since he believed other religions were of equal value if properly interpreted.[7]

> It was the New Testament which really awakened me to the rightness and value of Passive Resistance. When I read in the 'Sermon on the Mount', such passages as 'Resist not him that is evil, but whosoever smiteth thee on thy right cheek turn to him the other also', and 'Love your enemies and pray for them that persecute you, that ye may be sons of your Father which is in heaven', I was simply overjoyed, and found my own opinion confirmed where I least expected it. The 'Bhagavad Gita' deepened the impression, and Tolstoy's 'The Kingdom of God is Within You' gave it permanent form.[8]

Tolstoy's interpretation of the Sermon on the Mount

Gandhi had read Tolstoy's 'The Kingdom of God Is within You' when it had first appeared in the English translation in 1894.[9] In his writings Tolstoy had strongly criticised all Christian churches for perverting Christ's teachings, which he believed meant total pacifism. He ignored the Church Fathers' teaching on a 'just war' and believed that in the Sermon on the Mount Christ had condemned all violence. This made a deep impression on Gandhi.

In 1909 he wrote to Tolstoy, asking for permission to translate into Gujarati his 'Letter to a Hindoo', which had been published in English in an Indian newspaper, *Free Hindustan*. A considerable correspondence then developed between them, ending only with Tolstoy's death in 1910.

In his introduction to his translation of Tolstoy's 'Letter to a Hindoo' Gandhi wrote of him, 'Tolstoy's life has been devoted to replacing the method of violence for removing tyranny . . . He would meet hatred expressed in violence by love expressed in self-suffering.'[10] He explained his method of resistance:

> If we do not want the English in India, we must pay the price. Tolstoy indicates it . . . 'participate not in evil, in the violent deeds of the administration of the law courts, the collection of taxes and, what is more important, of the soldiers, and no one in the world will enslave you.'[11]

Practising satyagraha in South Africa

It was in this spirit that in 1909 Gandhi used his method of satyagraha for the first time to protest against the new law imposed by the government of the Transvaal, forcing the Indian population there to register and carry passes. Declaring they were being discriminated against, Gandhi urged Indians at a mass meeting to burn their passes or not register. As a result of their doing so, many were arrested and jailed, as was Gandhi. However, so great was the public outcry at their treatment that the Transvaal government had to negotiate a compromise with him.

By the time Gandhi had left South Africa at the end of 1914, he had forced the South African government to concede to a number of his demands and had established the non-violent protest movement with which he changed the thinking of the world, not so much by writings but by a practical flesh-and-blood example of what could be achieved. It was because of this that the poet Rabindranath Tagore called him 'Great Soul'.

Return to India, Home Rule through satyagraha

In 1915 Gandhi arrived back in India, where he organised some local peaceful protests, which encouraged him to believe that satyagraha should be used to achieve Home Rule.[12]

In 1919 a demonstration of unarmed Indians amassed in Amritsar to protest against the Rowlatt Acts that allowed the British to imprison them without trial. The demonstration was illegal, but the Indians may not have known it. The British troops, led by General Dyer, opened fire on the unarmed crowd repeatedly, killing 379 persons and injuring about 1,137 more. The Indians' fury at their treatment by the British reached a boiling point throughout the country.

In contrast to the ugliness around him, Gandhi took the lead of the Indian nationalist movement and of its vehicle, the Indian National Congress, which was demanding Home Rule. He urged the Indians not to use violence against the British but instead to practise satyagraha by peaceful non-cooperation in order to convert the British to his cause.

It was Gandhi's great achievement to persuade so many Indians against the easier path of violence and to conduct their protests in a dignified peaceful way so that they did not harm the enemy. The British government never realised how lucky they were to be opposed by such a peace-loving nationalist leader. Instead the British foolishly jailed him for alleged conspiracy to overthrow their government in India. He was sent to prison in 1922 for six years but released in 1924 after an operation for appendicitis. Meanwhile his followers had given up his non-cooperation movement and Hindus and Muslims were fighting each other. Gandhi fasted until they stopped.

Support for untouchables

In 1925 Gandhi was elected president of the Indian National Congress. He campaigned against the British in India, against child marriages and against the treatment of the untouchables. He did their work of cleaning latrines and generally tried to exalt their status. He also wanted India to develop village democracies and a simple life based on handmade products, including homespun cloth. In his own distinctive clothes of a simple homespun shawl and loincloth he became an iconic image of the Indian nationalist movement.

Demand for independence – Salt March 1930

In 1929 the Indian National Congress declared that complete independence, not just Home Rule, was its goal. As part of their non-cooperation movement, Congress members decided not to pay taxes to the British. The Salt Tax, imposed by the British in the nineteenth century, had always been deeply resented by the Indians. Therefore in March 1930 Gandhi led his famous Salt March against the tax. After over a month's walking, joined by thousands of Indians, he reached the sea at Dandi. There he gathered a handful of evaporated salt and held it symbolically aloft in defiance of the British Empire. His supporters followed him and 'salt madness' swept India as contraband salt was made. Hundreds of Indians were imprisoned, including him. Nothing daunted, he asked his son to organise a march on the Dharasana salt works. Two and a half thousand Indians, in wave after wave, marched to the works to be confronted by hundreds of policemen, who beat them bloodily, killing two of them. As usual Gandhi and his supporters won the moral argument since they had not sunk to using violence, as had the British. International respect for Gandhi increased.

Because of the outcry on Gandhi's behalf the British had to release him and furthermore invited him to the Second Round Table conference in London in 1931 on the constitutional future of India. However, the conference failed partly owing to the religious and social divisions among the Indians.

In 1934 Gandhi resigned his seat in Congress, and political leadership was now taken over by Jawaharlal Nehru. Gandhi travelled around India like a holy man, looking at social ills. He published a newspaper, *Harijan*, commenting on social and economic problems and also explaining the spiritual dimension of satyagraha.

Spiritual dimension of satyagraha

For Gandhi satyagraha was far more than an outward, political protest: it was an inward, deeply spiritual experience for the protestor, aimed at converting and not coercing the oppressor by example. In *Harijan* he explained the rules for those who wanted to participate in his movement and thus be 'satyagrahi':

1   He must have a living faith in God, for He is his only Rock.
2   He must believe in truth and non-violence as his creed and therefore have faith in the inherent goodness of human nature which he expects to evoke by his truth and love expressed through his suffering.
3   He must be living a chaste life and be ready and willing for the sake of his cause to give up his life and his possessions.[13]

Gandhi also believed in the importance of prayer:

in all my trials . . . I can say God saved me. When every hope is gone, 'when helpers fail and comforts flee,' I find that help arrives somehow, from I know not where. Supplication, worship, prayer are no superstition . . . I have not the slightest doubt that prayer is an unfailing means of cleansing the heart of passions. But it must be combined with the utmost humility.[14]

Gandhi had done the groundwork for Indian independence, making the British realise that they would have to cede it, but it was the Second World War that acted as a catalyst and forced them to leave India.

Second World War – independence of India
1947 – Gandhi's death

Gandhi and the Indian National Congress opposed Britain's declaring war on Nazi Germany, about which they had not been consulted. Gandhi would have opposed the violence of war anyway. In 1942 he began a 'Quit India' campaign against the British, for which they imprisoned him. In contrast, Jinnah and the Muslim League supported Britain's war effort so that their demand for a Muslim state was sympathetically received. After the war Britain's coffers were drained. It could no longer afford to control the growing nationalist movement in India. Moreover the Labour Party with its decolonisation policy had come to power in Britain and the USA was pressing for India's independence. This was granted in 1947, when Lord Mountbatten went out to India and swiftly divided it into two states, India and Pakistan. A bloody conflict between the Hindus and the Muslims then broke out as they fled to the countries where the majority of the population was of their religion. Gandhi fasted for peace, which was eventually restored. However, in 1948 Gandhi's life was ironically ended by violence. He was shot by a Hindu fanatic who disagreed with the creation of Muslim Pakistan.

Gandhi's achievements

Gandhi played a vital role in India's independence, for which the Second World War was only the catalyst. His non-violent methods saved many lives, British as well as Indian. Independence without undue harm to the enemy, who should be converted to the cause, was his noble goal.

Gandhi aimed at more than Indian independence. He believed that his method of satyagraha was for all times and places the right way to resolve conflict. He was no mere theorist but a flesh-and-blood practitioner of his teachings. And indeed out of admiration for his outstanding example, some of the most distinguished leaders of resistance movements have adopted his form of protest. Among them have been Martin Luther King and the civil rights movement in the USA, Nelson Mandela and the early resistance movement to apartheid in South Africa (before civil resistance itself was made a criminal offence), Chief Albert Luthuli, the anti-apartheid activist who won the Nobel Prize for peace in 1960, Aung San Suu Kyi and the opposition to the Burmese dictatorship, Vaclav Havel and the Czech Velvet Revolution and many more.

Gandhi may not have said an 'eye for an eye will make the whole world blind' (there is no evidence for this) but his message was certainly a rejection of revenge. His satyagraha may not be effective in all situations. Indeed he was lucky that he was opposing the British and not the Afrikaners. Moreover, Gandhi's belief in reincarnation could have meant that he did not see death as final, as a Westerner might. Nevertheless his satyagraha was a world-transforming example of what a disciplined human being can rise to in the ugliest of situations. Perhaps the 'inherent goodness of human nature' of which he wrote enables others to recognise his nobility and want to emulate it rather than reach for the gun.

Today, in 2016, when the death toll in the civil war in Syria has reached over 200,000, and violent conflicts are taking place in other countries, Gandhi's peaceful methods of protest look particularly superior and civilised. Indeed their appeal to the noblest instincts in humankind is both global and eternal. There can be no doubt that Gandhi's ethical actions have not resulted in the reverse of his aims. Indeed they will illuminate the path for peaceful protestors forever throughout the world.

Notes

1 Nanda, B. R., *Mahatma Gandhi: A Biography* (New Delhi 1981), p. 7.
2 Brown, Judith M., Gandhi and Civilian Resistance in India 1917–47, in Roberts, Adam and Ash, Timothy Garton, *Civil Resistance and Power Politics* (Oxford 2009), p. 44.
3 Ibid., p. 46.
4 Gandhi, M. K., *An Autobiography* (London 2001), p. 76–8.
5 Gandhi, M. K., *Hind Swaraj*, at http://www.mkgganhi.org/swarajya/ch017.htm, 'Passive Resistance', p. 2.
6 Ibid., p. 4.
7 Nanda, op. cit., p. 67.
8 Ibid., p. 95.
9 Parel, Anthony J., 'Gandhi and Tolstoy', in Mathai, M. P., *Meditations on Gandhi* (New Delhi 2002), p. 97.
10 Tolstoy, Leo, *Letter to a Hindoo* (Natal 1910 reprint), p. 3.
11 Ibid., p. 4.
12 Brown, op. cit., p. 44.
13 Gandhi, M. K., Harijan (Poona, India, 25 March 1939), p. 64.
14 Gandhi, M. K., *An Autobiography* (London 2001), p. 80.

16 Nelson Mandela and reconciliation

The second person to be considered in this section is Nelson Mandela, whose leadership of South Africa after the ending of apartheid and his release from twenty-seven years in jail was an outstanding example of forgiveness and reconciliation. This helped avoid the bloodshed of revenge and led to his becoming the most admired and loved political leader in the world. He wrote in his autobiography,

> I knew people expected me to harbour anger towards whites. But I had none. In prison, my anger towards whites decreased, but my hatred for the system grew. I wanted South Africa to see that I loved even my enemies while I hated the system that turned us against one another.[1]

Mandela's personal example of loving his enemies and policy of reconciliation when apartheid ended produced only positive results. Its source was probably his religious faith.

Mandela's Christian faith

Throughout his life, as Mandela remarked to his close friend and former fellow inmate on Robben Island, Ahmed Kathrada, 'I never abandoned my Christian beliefs.'[2] However, he never said much publicly about them. In a letter to his daughter Maki from his prison cell on Robben Island, he wrote that he thought it was better to keep religious beliefs to oneself:

> As you know, I was baptised in the Methodist Church and was educated in Wesleyan schools – Clarkebury, Healdtown and at Fort Hare. I stayed at Wesley House. At Fort Hare I even became a Sunday School teacher. Even here I attend all church services and have enjoyed some of the sermons . . . from experience, it's far better, darling, to keep religious

beliefs to yourself. You may unconsciously offend a lot of people by trying to sell them ideas they regard as unscientific and pure fiction.[3]

Early influences

It was Mandela's mother who gave him his faith. She was one of four wives of a Thembu chief and uneducated. Nevertheless, she was a devout Christian, had Mandela baptised and sent him, in 1925 when he was seven, to a primary Methodist mission school, where his teacher gave him the name 'Nelson'.

Two years later Mandela's father died. The regent and chief of the Thembu people became his guardian. Mandela went to live in the royal household, where he was given a Christian upbringing with the crown prince, going regularly to church with the royal family.

The African National Congress

In 1941, at the age of twenty-three, he arrived in Johannesburg to train as a lawyer. In the city he saw fully for the first time the degrading treatment that the whites meted out to black Africans, having seized their land and forced them to work in exploitative, degrading conditions. He joined the African National Congress in 1944 to work for a fully democratic South Africa, the black people having no vote.

The ANC used only peaceful methods of protest at that time, as it followed the ideas of Gandhi, who had campaigned for fellow Indians against racial discrimination in South Africa during the first decade of the twentieth century.

After the Afrikaner Nationalists came to power in 1948 and imposed 'apartheid' in South Africa, anyone criticising the laws of segregation could be arrested as a communist, according to the Suppression of Communism of 1950.

Mandela soon became deputy president of the ANC, leading peaceful protests against the apartheid laws and being jailed briefly. He also qualified as a lawyer and set up the first all-black law firm with Oliver Tambo, helping to get opponents of apartheid of jail.

Mandela turns to violent resistance

Then in 1960, two events occurred that made Mandela decide that the ANC's principle of non-violence must be changed. The first was the shooting at Sharpeville of sixty-nine peaceful protestors against the pass laws by young, inexperienced policemen. The second was the subsequent banning of the ANC. This meant that even peaceful protests under the auspices of the organisation could result in jail sentences.

Mandela came to believe that Gandhi's ideas were not effective when dealing with the Afrikaners: 'In India, Gandhi had been dealing with a foreign power that ultimately was more realistic and far-sighted. That was not the case with the Afrikaners in South Africa.'[4] In 1961 he persuaded the ANC to agree to the setting up of 'Umkhonto we Sizwe' (MK for short) or the 'Spear of the Nation' as the military arm of the ANC. He was to be its commander-in-chief and its method was to be sabotage, which he believed would not cause loss of life and therefore make reconciliation between the races easier afterwards.[5]

The campaign began with the blowing up of electricity power stations. Mandela secretly went abroad to ask for support and gain military training. When he returned in 1962 he was arrested and eventually sentenced to life imprisonment.

Reconciliation

He remained in jail for twenty-seven years. Had he died there he would not have become the international hero that he did, for it was his leadership of reconciliation after his release and the collapse of the apartheid system that won him the world's admiration.

In jail among his many activities he had time for spiritual reflection and reading. For example, when his wife, Winnie, was also imprisoned, he wrote to encourage her by referring to a book by the Afrikaner C. J. Langenhoven, *Shadows of Nazareth*, concerning Christ's unjust trial.[6] He attended all the church services in prison.[7] He kept a desk diary, and this is one entry for 19 August 1986: 'Rev Peter Storey on Forgiveness'; and then for the next day: 'The Rev Peter Storey on The Lord's Prayer'.[8]

Indeed it was Mandela's forgiveness of his enemies after he was freed that won him the world's admiration, avoided much bloodshed in South Africa and set a lasting example of how to lead a country from conflict to peace.

We cannot know for certain whether Mandela's use of violent protest made a significant contribution to the ending of apartheid, but we do know that it was Mandela's desire for reconciliation that enabled him to lead South Africa to democracy peacefully. His setting up, with Archbishop Desmond Tutu and others, the Truth and Reconciliation Commission, to investigate the truth about alleged human rights abuses and attempt to dispense restorative justice; his calming the nation after the assassination by a white supremacist of Chris Hani (his probable heir apparent) by pointing out that it was an Afrikaner woman who called the police and gave them the assassin's car number; his inviting his former prison guards to his inauguration ceremony;[9] his giving a luncheon for the wives and widows of the leaders, both black and white, of the apartheid struggle[10] and other such acts were all part of a distinctive desire for reconciliation, which probably avoided civil war in South Africa.

Mandela's policy of reconciliation, like Gandhi's of non-violence, has had only positive effects, which reverberate internationally. Both men were deeply influenced by the teachings of Jesus Christ, as was Robert Schuman, to whom we shall now turn.

Notes

1 Mandela, Nelson, *Long Walk to Freedom* (London 1995), p. 680.
2 Mandela, Nelson, *Conversations with Myself* (London 2011), p. 53.
3 Ibid., p. 235.
4 Mandela, op. cit., p. 182.
5 Mandela, *Long Walk to Freedom*, p. 336.
6 Mandela, *Conversations with Myself*, p. 223.
7 Ibid., p. 235.
8 Ibid., p. 298.
9 Frost, Brian, *Struggling to Forgive* (London 1998), p. 5.
10 Ibid., p. 12.

17 Robert Schuman and forgiveness

The third leader to be considered whose policy was highly ethical, a major peacemaking achievement which did not backfire, is Robert Schuman, the 'founding father' of the European Union. Schuman was a devout Christian who wanted to find a way of avoiding war breaking out in Europe again. His policy ended the decades-long cycle of wars of revenge between Germany and France.

In 2012 the EU was awarded the Nobel Peace Prize for transforming Europe 'from a continent of wars to a continent of peace'.[1] At the ceremony applause broke out when the leaders of Germany and France stood up holding hands. However, of all those who helped to create the EU perhaps none would have been more personally deserving of the Nobel Peace Prize, had he been alive, than Robert Schuman himself. He was the French foreign minister when he founded the European Coal and Steel Community (ECSC), with the specific aim of avoiding war breaking out between Germany and France again. The ECSC, established in 1951, developed into the EEC, which later became the EU. Without Robert Schuman the EU probably would never have been established: thus he is known as 'the Father of the European Community'.

Political career and Christian faith

During the Second World War, Schuman, who had been a member of the French Chamber of Deputies, was arrested by the Gestapo, but he escaped and joined the Resistance. After the war he rose rapidly, becoming the prime minister of France 1947–48, and then the foreign minister. In this capacity, in 1950 he introduced the plan for the European Coal and Steel Community, which integrated the German and French coal and steel industries. Schuman was determined to bring about a lasting peace between the two countries. He was ideally suited to the task, because firstly, although a French citizen, he had been educated in German universities, was at home in both countries and spoke both languages fluently; secondly, as a devout Christian who had once intended to enter the priesthood, he understood the importance of forgiveness. Indeed during the Second World War, while on the run from the Gestapo he had astonished those hiding him by talking of the need for cooperation with Germany after hostilities had ended.[2]

Schuman was well aware of the evil effects of revenge. France's desire for it after the First World War in the form of the Versailles Treaty had humiliated Germany, forcing it to pay excessive compensation damages. This had paved the way for the rise of Hitler. Schuman wanted to avoid such a situation occurring again. He also had a dream which he later expressed in his book *Pour L'Europe* that a united Europe might be created according to Christian principles in the geographical area once known as Christendom.

The European Coal and Steel Community

Therefore in 1950 Robert Schuman worked with the civil servant Jean Monnet on his plan, which provided for the integration of the coal and steel industries of Germany and France so that as steel would be jointly produced, the production of weapons for war by one of them would be impossible.

East Germany was then under the control of the Soviet Union, but there were factors working in Schuman's favour. West Germany, led by Chancellor Adenauer, wanted to regain its sovereignty and trust from other nations, which was likely if it were part of such arrangement. Moreover, there had already been Nazi-enforced collaboration during the Second World War between the Lorraine iron ore mines and the Saar coalfields, which were close to each other across the Franco-German borders. A pattern of cooperation had thus already been established.

Schuman sprang the plan on the French Cabinet in May 1950, demanding an instant response before opposition could be organised. Some of the Cabinet members, such as the prime minister, Georges Bidault, were thinking in terms of a Franco-American alliance and needed persuading, but eventually Schuman won them over, partly because the idea of France taking the initiative in European affairs appealed to the French Cabinet. Few of its members could, however, have envisaged the momentous consequences of their decision.

West Germany agreed to the Schuman Plan, which, on 9 May 1950, Schuman revealed to the world. He declared that the coming together of the nations of Europe 'requires the elimination of the age-old opposition of France and Germany'. The plan proposed that Franco-German production of coal and steel be placed under a common High Authority, within a framework open to the participation of the other countries of Europe. It would be 'a first step in the federation of Europe'.[3]

Italy, Belgium, the Netherlands and Luxembourg had also been invited to join the project, to which they agreed. However, Britain refused to participate as it wanted to preserve its independence and believed it had a special relationship with the USA and that, together with the Commonwealth, was sufficient for its needs.

In 1951 the European Coal and Steel Community was set up with the six members, forming a common market in coal and steel. Supranational institutions were set up to govern it, consisting of the High Authority, Council of Ministers, Parliament and Court.

The European Economic Community

So successful was the ECSC that its six members decided to enlarge it into the European Economic Community in 1957. This was a common market of all their goods and services, with free movement of workers and capital. Its political institutions were to be a commission to make proposals for the EEC as a whole, a council of ministers from members states who could veto these proposals, a parliament of representatives from members states' national assemblies and an independent court.

Despite setbacks, the EU has flourished economically until recently and has buttressed the new democracies in Southern and Eastern Europe. Above all there has been peace between Germany and France, and peace is likely to last between all the members of the EU so long as they remain in economic cooperation.

As for Schuman, he was appointed the first president of the European Parliamentary Assembly from 1958 to 1960, which awarded him the title of 'Founding Father of Europe'. He died in 1963, aged seventy-seven, having seen what may well be a permanent peace forged between France and its former enemy, Germany.

A united Europe

To avoid conflicts such as that in Ukraine (in 2014), Schuman would no doubt have wanted the EU to expand to include Russia (which, with Belarus, Kazakhstan, Kyrgyzstan and Armenia, formed the Eurasian Economic Union in 2015). The collaboration of the two unions would result in the peaceful, prosperous economic and democratic development of both Eastern and Western Europe, with the abundance of raw materials in Russia in particular, whose democratic institutions would be firmly buttressed.

Such a united Europe, which could play a strong role globally for peace, would fully realise Robert Schuman's dream. Moreover, his idea that states which were former enemies could work together for their economic and political good might well be copied in the Middle East and elsewhere to the advantage of the whole world. Forgiveness of former enemies and a willingness to cooperate with them never backfires but brings only positive results.

Schuman's and Mandela's policies of forgiveness, like Gandhi's practice of non-violent resistance, have had only positive effects, which reverberate internationally. All three men were greatly influenced by the teachings of Jesus Christ. It is a tragedy that His birthplace, the Middle East, has not yet produced a modern leader who can guide the people there to forgiveness, reconciliation and peace.

Notes

1 www.bbc.co.uk/news/world-europe, 12 October 2012.
2 Mowat, R. C., *Creating the European Community* (London 1973), p. 44.
3 http://europa.eu/about-eu/basic-information/symbols/Europe-day/schuman-declaration.

Conclusion

In this book I have considered how extremely unethical policies have frequently produced unwanted results; indeed many have been the reverse of those intended.

I began by considering Israel's treatment of the Palestinians, which, far from making it more secure, has produced the completely opposite result. The West's involvement in Iran, Iraq, Afghanistan and Libya has been of dubious morality and has not achieved the intended aims – often the reverse. In China and Russia, extremely harsh policies have had consequences that were the antithesis of those which were wanted. Although there might be a time lag, the link between the policy and result can be traced. Similarly the Second World War showed how revenge is counterproductive. The Nazis' attempt to destroy the Jews produced completely the reverse results. Genocide failed in the former state of Yugoslavia, too, though not with such spectacular, antithetical consequences. However, there have been examples of where genocide did not seem to backfire onto the perpetrators. I consider these and examples of Western imperialism where the results do not seem to be the reverse of what were intended.

I conclude that the rule of reverse results does not seem to apply to every unethical policy. But the frequency with which it does so results in a rule of increased likelihood, whereas an extremely ethical policy is less likely to backfire.

A government needs to protect its security, commercial and strategic interests, but if this involves invading another country and killing its citizens without UN authorisation, this is clearly unethical. The motivation behind policies determines whether they are immoral, such as those driven by revenge, greed, power, glory, racism and self-interested pressure groups.

On the other hand there are some policies that are clearly ethical and even if taken to extremes do not cause any reverse results. These are the policies of non-violent protest as practised by Gandhi in India, reconciliation as encouraged by Mandela in South Africa, and forgiveness as implemented by Schuman as France's foreign policy towards Germany. Moreover, these leaders, by their ethical policies, prevented the rule of reverse results, which would have been in the form of a backlash, from playing out in their countries.

I have indicated in this book that besides eschewing illegal invasions, the ethical principles that governments should practise in their foreign policies to avoid reverse results are: forgiveness instead of violent revenge, persistent diplomacy to avoid war, care for the poor and the right to protect the vulnerable. I shall now consider them in the light of the argument of this book, beginning with forgiveness. This is not the denial of justice but of revenge, which is always disproportionate and unconstructive.

Forgiveness

In the history of the twentieth century it is clear that forgiveness could have saved millions of lives. An important factor that caused the rise of Hitler and the Second World War was France's desire for revenge after the humiliation of its defeat in the Franco-Prussian War of 1871. The harsh terms of the Versailles Treaty in 1919 meant that many Germans supported Hitler, who vowed to repudiate the treaty. Had France shown forgiveness to Germany in 1919 and made a generous peace treaty, Hitler might never have come to power. There then would have been no Holocaust, nor German invasion of France in 1940.

After the Second World War, the French foreign minister, Robert Schuman, knew that the way forward was France's forgiveness of Germany and the building of the EU. It is not possible to know if this alone has caused the lasting peace between France and Germany but it certainly has played a major role, which justified its being awarded the Nobel Peace Prize.

Today the absence of forgiveness in the Middle East, the cycle of revenge attacks between the Israelis and the Palestinians, lasting for over sixty years, shows the futility of mere vengeance, which unfortunately is still a matter of honour in many countries. Israel's policy towards the Palestinian people is still resulting in its continual insecurity: an outcome the opposite of that intended.

Meanwhile in the more recent conflict in Syria there is no high-minded response from any side which might lead to peace (at the time of writing in early 2016). For some reason the Middle East has not produced a Gandhi, Schuman or Mandela: it needs to do so in order to avoid the sinister unintended results of ill-thought-out military action.

Between the USA and Libya there was a cycle of revenge resulting probably in the tragedy of the Lockerbie bombing and then of the overthrow of Gaddafi. Al-Qaeda's attack on the USA in 2001 may well have been an act of revenge, but this is also what the USA's response may have been in Afghanistan.

Revenge attacks used to take place regularly in Northern Ireland, but the fact that there is now peace there, however fragile, gives cause for hope that other cycles of revenge will end. One man who pointed the way there to forgiveness and reconciliation was Gordon Wilson. He was a Northern Ireland Protestant who in 1987 immediately forgave the IRA bombers who had just killed his daughter, along with ten other people, by a lethal explosion at a Remembrance Day ceremony in Enniskillen. The Queen later remarked in her Christmas broadcast that he had impressed the whole world with the depth of his forgiveness. Indeed at such times one can see that man is ascending and not descending from animals and human life is moving to a higher, nobler level. As Alexander Pope pithily observed, 'To err is human / To forgive divine'.[1]

Persistent diplomacy

The second principle that voters should demand that their government implement in foreign policy is that of persistent, patient diplomacy. No good comes from closing doors to others, expelling ambassadors and shutting embassies. The electorate should urge their governments to persist with diplomacy and hospitality for putative enemies. Indeed, even though it may be difficult to engender trust, respect can nevertheless be built up through patient negotiations. Humour should be particularly valued in persons chosen to negotiate as it has been shown to generate creativity and thus problem solving.[2] This form of diplomacy would prevent the unintended adverse results of unethical policies. In truth, it could create peace.

If politicians meet physically, the exchanges are usually more creative and productive. A good example of this occurred in 2013 when there seemed little hope of Western leaders holding face-to-face meetings about the civil war in Syria with its ally Russia. Instead the USA proposed punitive air-strikes against the Syrian regime for allegedly using chemical weapons against a rebel-held area in Damascus.

Then in September 2013 in Moscow, at a conference of the G20, which was not meant to be about Syria, the leaders of Russia, the USA, the UK and other states did discuss the USA's proposed air-strikes against Syria. The suggestion was made that Assad could hand over the chemical weapons to an international authority. Russia took up the idea and got President Assad to agree to it.

The conversation on the sidelines, as the G20 meeting was not about Syria, played a pivotal role in finding a solution to the impasse over Syria's chemical weapons. It shows the importance of foreign ministers physically meeting and sparking off ideas, sometimes not about the subject for which they were convened. Assad might not have given up his nuclear weapons but for the G20 conference.

Reduction of poverty

The third principle that voters should demand of their government's foreign policy is the reduction of poverty, illiteracy and disease in developing countries, which helps to avoid the development of extremism. In the twentieth century poverty was one of the main reasons why people supported communism, with its offerings of full employment, free health and free education to university level as well as cheap housing. One reason for the popularity of Hezbollah, Hamas and the Muslim Brotherhood is that these organisations also provide free social services, including hospitals and schools. The West needs to alleviate poverty in the developing countries if it is to forestall Islamic extremism there.

The right to protect

The fourth principle, the right to protect, is a controversial one. This was endorsed by the UN General Assembly at the 2005 World Summit and can be traced back to 1999, when the British prime minister Tony Blair, in a speech at the Economic Club of Chicago, invoked such a principle to justify NATO's intervention in Kosovo, where it was successful.

In his speech Blair propounded what he called a 'Doctrine of the International Community': 'a rather grand title for what was really a very simple notion: intervention to bring down a despotic dictatorial regime could be justified on grounds of the nature of that regime, not merely its immediate threat to our interests.'[3] The principle became known as the Responsibility to Protect or R2P. Blair set out five major considerations to be taken into account before intervention:

> First are we sure of our case? War is an imperfect instrument for righting humanitarian distress; but armed force is sometimes the only means of dealing with dictators. Second, have we exhausted all diplomatic options? We should always give peace every chance, as we have in the case of Kosovo. Third, on the basis of a practical assessment of the situation, are there military operations that we can prudently undertake?

Fourth, are we prepared for the long term? In the past we talked too much of exit strategies. But having made a commitment we cannot simply walk away once the fight is over; better to stay with moderate numbers of troops than return for repeat performances with large numbers. And finally, do we have national interests involved?[4]

An opportunity to show that these criteria could be met and the principle of Responsibility to Protect could be carried out successfully arose the following year. In May 2000 Tony Blair authorised the military intervention of British troops in Sierra Leone. There the democratically elected government was threatened by the rampage of brutal gangsters called the Revolutionary United Front (RUF), who were committing atrocities against civilians and plundering the country's resources. The intervention was successful as well as ethical because it saved lives and was requested by the democratically elected president. It did not backfire on Britain or Sierra Leone.

When in 2005 the UN General Assembly endorsed the principle of Responsibility to Protect, some commentators saw this as a progressive step whereby the international community would prevent massacres. However, after NATO's intervention in Libya in 2011, ostensibly to protect the people of Benghazi, this hope seemed to be ill-founded. The intervention led to regime change, chaos, violence and the near disintegration of the Libyan state. Nevertheless it could be argued that the military intervention did not meet any of Blair's criteria for R2P and greatly exceeded its remit.

Often a conflict is not between the clearly good and clearly bad. Obviously if all the UN Security Council members agree on such a policy to intervene, it is unlikely to be either unethical or counterproductive. Unfortunately consensus is often difficult to achieve. However, action to protect does not necessarily mean arms. It should surely be possible for the UN to devise a way of protecting the lives of civilians not only by military means but also by a rapid reaction force to transport them away from war-torn areas to places of safety.

In this book I have argued that unethical policies, unlike ethical policies, are highly likely to produce results that are the reverse of those intended. This is another reason, besides avoiding the loss of life and resources, for citizens to urge their politicians, who often make policies on the hoof and do not see the bigger picture, to avoid such actions.

In a democracy we are responsible for our government's foreign policy in a way that those living under dictatorships are not. We have not only the right but also the democratic and ethical duty to oppose peacefully our government's pursuing policies of dubious legality and morality.

A government that practises forgiveness, persistent diplomacy in place of war, aims for the reduction of global poverty and supports the UN's actions to protect the vulnerable is less likely to find that its policies backfire, wasting lives and funds. We can never predict with certainty the outcome of governmental decisions, but these aforementioned ethical policies are most likely to benefit all concerned and most unlikely to have harmful, unintended consequences.

Notes

1 Pope, Alexander, 'An Essay on Criticism', in *Selected Poetry* (Oxford 1998), p. 14, line 525.
2 Goddard, Vaughan, 'The Effect of a Humorous Atmosphere upon the Facilitation of Creativity in an Organisational Context', MSc Thesis (University of Surrey 1995).
3 Blair, Tony, *A Journey* (London 2010), p. 247.
4 Ibid., p. 248.

Select Bibliography

Primary sources and articles

Akhmatova, Anna, http://www.poemhunter.com/poem/requiem.

Azzam, Abdullah, 'Defence of the Muslim Lands', www.religioscope.com.

The Battle of Britain Historical Society, www.battleofbritain1940.net.

BBC World News, http://www.bbc.co.uk/news/.

BBC World News, www.bbc.co.uk/history/worldwars/wwtwo/areabombing.

Bellasco, Amy, Congressional Research Service, 29 March 2011, www.crs.gov.

British Mandate, A Survey of Palestine prepared by the British Mandate for the UN, Vol. 1, http://www.palestineremembered.com/articles/a-survey-of-palestine/story6628.html.

Christian Science Monitor, www.csmonitor.com/2003/1104/p11s01-legn.html.

'Countries Slam Western Air Raids against Libya', *People's Daily*, Online, 22 March 2011, http://english.people.com.cn/90001/90777/90855/7327318.html.

CNN, http//archives.cnn.co.

The Daily Mail (London).

The Daily Express (London).

Dawn, www.dawn.com.

Deccan Chronicle, www.deccanchronicle.com.

Deng, Xiaoping, *Selected Works of Deng Xiaoping (1975–1982)*, Vol. 2 (Beijing 1984).

Deng, Xiaoping, *Selected Works of Deng Xiaoping (1982–1992)*, Vol. 3 (Beijing 1994).

Europa, http://europa.eu/about-eu/basic-information/symbols/Europe-day/schuman-declaration.

Gaidar, Yegor, Speech, www.aei.org/issue/foreign-and-defense-policy/regional/europe/the-soviet-collapse.

Gallica, www.gallica.bnf.fr.

Gandhi, M. K., *Harijan* (Poona, India 1939).

Gasiorowski, Mark, 'The 1953 Coup d'Etat in Iran', *International Journal of Middle East Studies*, Vol. 19, No. 3 (Aug 1987), pp. 261–286.

Global Security, http://www.globalsecurity.org/military/world/russia/mo-budget.htm.

Goddard, Vaughan, 'The Effect of a Humorous Atmosphere upon the Facilitation of Creativity in an Organisational Context', MSc Thesis (University of Surrey 1995).

The Guardian (London).

The History Guide, www.historyguide.org/europe/churchill.html.
Hitler Historical Museum, http://www.hitler.org/writings/meinkampf/mkulch11.html.
Holocaust History, http://www.holocaust-history.org.
House of Commons Hansard Debates, www.publications.parliament.uk.
House of Lords Hansard Debates, www.publications.parliament.uk.
The Huffington Post (New York), www.huffingtonpost.com.
iCasualties, www.icasualties.org/OEF.
The Independent (London).
Jewish Virtual Library, http://www.jewishvirtuallibrary.org/isource/history.
Kramarenko, Alexander, Minister Counsellor of the Embassy of Russia to Great Britain, Lecture to the Great Britain-Russia Society, 30 October 2013.
Letter from President to the Speaker of the House of Representatives, March 18, 2003, http://georgewbush-whitehouse.archives.gov/news/releases/2003/03/print/ 20030319–1.
l'express, http://www.lexpress.fr/actualite/politique/bhl-assassine-juppe.
Mandela, Nelson, Speech at the Zionist Christian Church Easter Conference 1992, http://www.anc.org.za/,
Manningham-Buller, Eliza, 'Reith Lectures', www.bbc.co.uk/reithlectures.
NBC News, www.nbcnews.com.
The New York Times (New York), www.nytimes.com.
People's Daily Online (Beijing), http://english.people.com.
Politikalblog, 'GaddafisFatefulSpeech',http://thepolitikalblog.wordpress.com/2011/ 12/9/gaddafis-fateful-speech
President Gorbachev's speech to the Council of Europe, Strasbourg, 6 July 1989, http://www.pro-europa.eu.
The Progressive Review, http://www.prorev.com.
The Telegraph (London).
The Times (London).
UN Human Development Report 2010, hdr.undp.org.
USA Office of National Intelligence, http://www.dni.gov.
Vox, www.vox.com/2014/6/20/5824480/why-the-iraqi-army-cant-defeat-isis.
Washington Post (Washington, D.C.).
'Who the US Should Really Hit in ISIS and Casualties in Iraq', 23 September 2014, Caerusassociates.com/news.
The World Today-Chatham House (London).

Index

For Product Safety Concerns and Information please contact our EU
representative GPSR@taylorandfrancis.com
Taylor & Francis Verlag GmbH, Kaufingerstraße 24, 80331 München, Germany

www.ingramcontent.com/pod-product-compliance
Ingram Content Group UK Ltd.
Pitfield, Milton Keynes, MK11 3LW, UK
UKHW021423080625
459435UK00011B/139